BRILLIANT INSIGHTS INTO THE HUMAN PSYCHE

Carl Jung is second only to Sigmund Freud among the giants of modern psychological thought. Starting out as Freud's most important disciple, Jung soon broke away from his mentor to follow his own lines of investigation and discovery, blazing new trails in a long lifetime of unceasing activity.

Many of Jung's ideas are now fundamental to our understanding of the mysteries of the mind. Other more controversial theories dealing with the psychological relevance of such phenomena as occultism, astrology, alchemy, and extrasensory perception are only now being considered in the light of their possible importance. Here, in one stimulating volume, are the brilliant contributions to the study of human behavior by one of the prime innovators of modern thought.

CALVIN S. HALL and VERNON J. NORDBY are members of the staff of the University of California, Santa Cruz, where they have collaborated in the field of dream research. They are co-authors of THE INDIVIDUAL AND HIS DREAMS.

Dr. Hall, Senior Lecturer in Psychology and Fellow of Cowell College, is also author or co-author of a number of other books, including THE CONTENT ANALYSIS OF DREAMS, THEORIES OF PERSONALITY, and A PRIMER OF FREUDIAN PSYCHOLOGY.

A PRIMER OF
Jungian Psychology

By
CALVIN S. HALL
and
VERNON J. NORDBY

A MENTOR BOOK

MENTOR
Published by the Penguin Group
Penguin Books USA Inc., 375 Hudson Street,
New York, New York 10014, U.S.A.
Penguin Books Ltd, 27 Wrights Lane,
London W8 5TZ, England
Penguin Books Australia Ltd, Ringwood,
Victoria, Australia
Penguin Books Canada Ltd, 10 Alcorn Avenue,
Toronto, Ontario, Canada M4V 3B2
Penguin Books (N.Z.) Ltd, 182–190 Wairau Road,
Auckland 10, New Zealand

Penguin Books Ltd, Registered Offices:
Harmondsworth, Middlesex, England

Published by Mentor, an imprint of Dutton Signet,
a division of Penguin Books USA Inc.

First Printing, May, 1973
21 20 19 18 17 16

REGISTERED TRADEMARK—MARCA REGISTRADA

Library of Congress Catalog Card Number: 72-96011

Printed in the United States of America

THIS PRIMER IS DEDICATED TO OUR
WISE AND GOOD JUNGIAN FRIENDS,
C. A. MEIER OF ZURICH AND JO
WHEELWRIGHT OF SAN FRANCISCO,
AND TO THE MEMORY OF C. G. JUNG.

Preface

A Primer of Freudian Psychology was published in 1954. This book was written to introduce students and the public to Freud's ideas about the structure, dynamics, and development of the *normal* personality. Evidently it has served the purpose for which it was written, as it has been read by a very large number of people since its publication.

For many years, we have wanted to write a similar introduction to the psychological views of C. G. Jung. We hesitated, however, because we felt there would not be much of an audience for such a book. Except for an interest in Jung's word-association experiments conducted in the early 1900's, which earned him an invitation from psychologists to lecture in the United States (1909), and a subsequent interest in devising tests for measuring Jung's concepts of introversion and extraversion, American psychologists, and psychologists in other countries as well, have paid little attention to this Swiss psychologist and psychiatrist who died in 1961. When they have considered his ideas at all it has usually been to reject them. Their criticisms have sometimes been justified, but more often they have been based on a misunderstanding of Jung.

Part of the fault lies with Jung himself. He was a discursive writer, which often makes it difficult to follow the train of his thought. Moreover, his writings discourage many readers by their erudition regarding topics of which few people have much knowledge and in which they have little interest.

Within the last few years, a positive interest in Jung's psychology has begun to develop, especially among younger psychologists, students, and the general public. They believe he has something significant to say about human behavior. So do we. We think Jung is one of the prime innovators or movers of modern thought; to ignore him is to lose ideas that are very pertinent to these troubled times. That is why we have written this book. We hope it will serve the same purpose for Jung that *A Primer of Freudian Psychology* has for Freud: to introduce the reader to the basic Jungian concepts concerning the structure, dynamics, and development of the *normal* personality.

Like the Freud primer, this book is purely expository. We have tried to present Jung's concepts and theories clearly, simply, and accurately. We have not attempted to evaluate or criticize his ideas, nor have we compared them with those of other psychologists and psychoanalysts. We have omitted from consideration Jung's views on abnormal behavior (the neuroses and psychoses) and psychotherapy. Nor have we discussed the work of other Jungian psychologists and psychiatrists who have added to the body of analytical psychology.

We have used only the published works of Jung in writing this primer. They have been translated into English and are available in a nineteen-volume edition published by the Princeton University Press. All citations, unless otherwise noted, are to this edition of Jung's *Collected Works* (see page 135). We hope this primer will encourage our readers to consult these original sources.

CALVIN S. HALL

VERNON J. NORDBY

Santa Cruz, California
July, 1972

Contents

A PRIMER OF
Jungian Psychology

CHAPTER ONE

Carl Gustav Jung
(1875-1961)

"My life is a story of the self-realization of the unconscious."

In 1957, when Carl Jung was eighty-two years old, he began to write his autobiography in collaboration with his personal secretary, Aniela Jaffé. The result of this collaboration, published in 1961, the year of Jung's death, under the title *Memories, Dreams, Reflections,* is an astonishingly candid assessment of the forces and influences that shaped his intellectual development. Instead of giving an objective account of his life—although there is some of that, too—Jung chose to analyze and describe his subjective or inner life, a world of dreams, visions, and spiritual experiences.

We have drawn generously from this unique source in writing the following brief account of Jung's life. There is an emphasis on childhood experiences because these were, so Jung thought, decisive in forming his character, attitudes, and interests. We have not slighted the biographical facts, however, because we feel that the reader will want to know who Jung was and what he did.

I. CHILDHOOD AND YOUTH

Carl Gustav Jung, named for his illustrious grandfather, a professor of medicine at the University of Basel, was born on July 26, 1875, in the small village of Kesswil on Lake Constance in the northeastern part of Switzerland. He was the oldest child and only surviving son of a Swiss Reform pastor. Two brothers died in infancy before Jung was born.

When Jung was six months old his father was assigned to a parish in Laufen, another small village located on the Rhine river. It was here that Jung's mother developed a nervous disorder, probably as a result of marital difficulties, which required her to be hospitalized for several months. The young boy was placed under the supervision of an elderly aunt and the family maid.

The aunt showed Jung his first view of the awesome Alps from the parsonage. The Alps intrigued him and he insisted on going to them at once, but the aunt prevailed on him to postpone the journey. Mountains, lakes, and rivers were, and still are, the natural habitat of any Swiss child. "Without water," Jung observed, "nobody could live at all." Despite his highly developed intellectual life, Jung always remained close to nature.

Death, also, was no stranger to him. Quite often local fishermen were killed in the vicious waterfall, and Jung recalled vividly the funeral rites: a large black box beside a deep hole, the services conducted by clergymen garbed in black coats and tall black hats, their faces somber and cold. Besides his father, eight of his uncles were parsons, so Jung as a boy spent considerable time around black-frocked, sober men. For many years their appearance inspired fear in the boy.

The next and last parish the Jung family moved to was in Klein-Hüningen, a village on the Wiese River about three miles from Basel. Once the dam burst, causing a flood that drowned fourteen people. After the flood subsided the adventurous Jung, now six years old, ran outside to investigate the damage and discovered the corpse of a man half-buried in the sand. On another occasion he watched a pig being slaughtered and butchered. These experiences were extremely exciting for him, but perplexing to his mother, who thought it was unhealthy for a young boy to take an interest in such morbid events.

Jung himself had some close brushes with death while a boy. Once he cracked his head open and bled all over the church steps. Another time he nearly plunged to his death from the bridge crossing the Rhine falls, being rescued at the last moment by the family maid.

Jung played by himself, since his sister was not born until he was nine. He spent hours inventing and playing games, then abandoning them to devise new and more complex ones. He could not tolerate criticism or on-lookers, nor did he want anyone to disturb him or to interfere while he played. Jung was not enthusiastic about the newborn sister; he ignored her presence and continued to play by himself. Jung was an introvert then and remained so throughout his life.

Jung's parents had marriage problems ever since the child could remember, and they slept in separate bedrooms. Jung shared a bedroom with his father. He recalls hearing the strange and, to him, mysterious noises his mother made during the night. The sounds upset him, and he often had terrifying dreams. In one dream he saw a figure coming through his mother's door. The head became detached from the body and floated in the air. Then another head appeared, only to become detached again and float away.

Jung's father was often irritable and difficult to get along with; his mother suffered from emotional disorders and depressions. When these conditions became more than he could tolerate, Jung sought refuge in the attic. There he had a companion to console and comfort him, a manikin he had carved from a piece of wood. The manikin provided Jung with endless hours of ceremonies and rituals; secret pacts and miniature scrolls were hidden along with it in the attic. Jung carried on lengthy conversations with the manikin and divulged his innermost secrets to it.

When Jung was eleven years old he transferred from the village school to a large school in the city of Basel. Here he was exposed to a much wealthier class of people than he had ever imagined existed. The Basel gentlemen lived in stately mansions, spoke refined German and French, and drove beautifully decorated carriages drawn by magnificent horses. Their sons, possessing fine manners, stylish clothes, and abundant pocket money, were Jung's new classmates. These affluent boys spoke of vacations in the Alps, on Lake Zurich, and other places Jung longed to visit. The impoverished parson's son who attended classes in rain-soaked socks and worn-out shoes was envious of his schoolmates. Jung developed a different feeling about his parents, and even began to feel some compassion for his father, a feeling previously far remote. He had not realized before how poor his father was.

School soon became tedious and required far too much time which Jung felt could be spent reading about subjects that really interested him. He found divinity classes especially dull, and abhorred any type of mathematics. He loathed gymnastics, from which he was excused when he developed fainting spells. These neurotic attacks increased in frequency, and he missed more than six months of school. During this absence he indulged in the pleasures he valued above all else, the freedom to read what he wanted to read and to explore nature. He plunged into the mysterious world of trees, stones, animals, swamps—and his father's library.

Jung's parents were concerned about their son's fainting spells and consulted one physician after another. The disorder remained undiagnosed, although one specialist suggested it might be epilepsy, and the remedies prescribed were without effect. Jung was in total bliss, and did not give the condition serious thought until he overheard his father talking to a friend who had inquired about the boy's health. "The doctors no longer know what is wrong with him. It would be dreadful if he were incurable. I have lost what little I had, and what will become of the boy if he cannot earn his living?" Jung was thunderstruck; reality suddenly hit him in the face. From that moment the illness disappeared, never to return. He immediately ran into his father's library and began refreshing his knowledge of Latin grammar. He resumed going to school and studied more diligently than he had ever thought possible. Jung says he really learned what a neurosis was from this experience.

From early childhood Jung had dreams, experiences, and feelings he dared not tell anyone. Questions concerning religion were taboo. "One ought to believe and have faith" was the reply Jung received whenever he questioned a religious concept. Religion was not the only subject that produced confusion in Jung's mind, but it was the barrier that made communication with his father virtually impossible. Jung described his childhood as one of almost unendurable loneliness. "Thus the pattern of my relationship to the world was already prefigured; today as then I am a solitary" (*Memories, Dreams, Reflections*, hereafter abbreviated as MDR, p. 41).

Jung's religious conflicts persisted throughout adolescence. He searched unsuccessfully through books for answers to his questions. When this preoccupation became tiresome he would escape from it by reading poetry, drama, and history. Religious discussions with his father invariably ended unsatisfactorily, often with fuss and hard feelings. These acrimonious debates saddened and irritated the pastor, who ironically succumbed to a much more serious religious conflict in his later years than his son ever experienced.

Despite his theological concerns, Jung devoted ample time to his studies, and succeeded in becoming first in his class. After his sixteenth year the religious dilemma was slowly displaced by other interests, especially philosophy. The thoughts of the Greek philosophers attracted Jung, but his favorite was Schopenhauer, who dealt with suffering, confusion, passion, and evil. Here at last, Jung thought, was a philosopher courageous enough to confess that not all of the fundaments of the universe are for the best. Schopenhauer depicted life as he saw it, and he did not camouflage the undesirable features of humanity. This philosophical message gave Jung a fresh perspective on life.

During this time Jung changed from a reserved, mistrustful person to a more aggressive, communicative person. Feeling more self-confident, he initiated a number of friendships and even divulged some of his thoughts and opinions to his new friends. His ideas were met with mockery and hostility. Jung finally realized why the other students rebuked him. He read extensively on subjects that were not assigned in the classroom, thus acquiring knowledge that was foreign to the other students. When he discoursed on these topics his classmates, incapable of understanding them, thought he was an impostor who spun theories and ideas out of his own imagination. Some of his teachers accused him of plagiarism. Jung once again felt alienated, and retreated into himself.

The picture that Jung draws of himself during his youth is that of a solitary, bookish intellectual, puzzled by religious and philosophical questions and curious about the world. He was certainly no ordinary boy, just as he was to become no ordinary man. Yet many a boy of his temperament never develops into anything extraordinary. They often remain immature, become neurotic, or fritter away their lives in eccentricities.

II. PROFESSIONAL ACTIVITIES

Nearing completion of high school, Jung was asked by his parents what career he intended to follow. Jung did not know. He was interested in a diversity of subjects, but he was not ready to commit himself to any specific subject at this point. The concrete facts of science attracted him, but so did comparative religion and philosophy. One of his uncles strongly encouraged theology, but Jung's father dissuaded him from that choice.

With time drawing near for Jung to enroll at the university, he still had not decided on a profession. He was interested in four fields: science, history, philosophy, and archeology. Archeology was promptly eliminated because Basel University did not offer it, and Jung lacked the funds to study elsewhere. Science was finally chosen, and soon after he began attending classes it suddenly occurred to Jung that he could study medicine. It is strange that he had not thought of this before, because the grandfather for whom he was named had been a professor of medicine in the university where Jung was enrolled. Jung felt he resisted following his grandfather's profession because he was determined not to imitate anyone. Jung's father was able to provide a small portion of the tuition; the remainder was loaned by the university.

Jung's financial situation worsened when his father died a year after Jung had entered the university. This left him responsible for the support of his mother and sister. Some of the relatives urged Jung to discontinue his studies and seek employment. Fortunately, one uncle offered financial assistance to take care of the family, and other relatives loaned Jung money to continue at the university.

Upon completion of an anatomy course Jung was made a junior assistant, and the following semester he was placed in charge of the histology course. He still managed to find time to continue reading philosophy. During his third year Jung was trying to decide whether to specialize in surgery or internal medicine. He finally abandoned the idea of specialization because it would require additional education for which he did not have the money.

During the following summer vacation several occult experiences occurred which were to influence Jung's vocational choice. Dreams, fantasies, and parapsychological phenomena were always to play a great role in Jung's life, especially when he had to make an important decision. Even as a boy he had begun to take seriously manifestations of the unconscious mind, especially as revealed in dreams.

The first mysterious experience happened one day when Jung was in his room studying. Suddenly he heard a loud noise like a pistol shot. He went into the next room, where his mother was sitting about three feet from the large dinner table. The table was split from the rim to the center through solid wood and not along any joint or seam. It was made of aged walnut, and the splitting could not have been caused by a change in temperature or humidity. Jung was baffled.

The second experience took place one evening. This time it was a large bread knife lying in a bread basket that had shattered into several pieces. Jung took the pieces to a cutler, who exclaimed after examining them, "This knife was perfectly sound; there is no fault in the steel. Someone must have deliberately broken it piece by piece." Many years later when Jung's wife was fatally ill, Jung took the pieces from a safe and had them mounted as a whole knife.

Shortly after these events, Jung began attending séances and table turnings which were held at the home of relatives every Saturday night. His interest in the occult never diminished, and for his doctoral dissertation he investigated the behavior of a medium, a fifteen-year-old girl who performed at the séances of his relatives.

These mysterious phenomena were instrumental in turning Jung's interest to psychology and psychopathology. That fall when he returned to the university he read a textbook on psychiatry by Krafft-Ebing in preparation for his final examinations. The first chapter struck him like a bolt of lightning; he knew immediately that psychiatry was his destined field. In his twenty-fourth year, then, Jung had finally found the field that was compatible with his interests, speculations, and ambitions. Everything fell into place.

His professors were dismayed by his decision. They were astonished that he would sacrifice a promising medical career for such an absurd field as psychiatry. The medical profession generally was contemptuous of psychiatry; they thought it a lot of nonsense and considered the psychiatrist as peculiar as the patients he treated. Jung characteristically held a firm position on his choice.

On December 10, 1900, Jung assumed his first professional appointment as assistant at the Burghölzli Mental Hospital in Zurich. Burghölzli was the most famous mental hospital in Europe. Its director was Eugen Bleuler, who was world-famous for his treatment of psychoses and his development of the concept of schizophrenia. Jung recognized his good fortune in having the opportunity to study and work under such a famous man.

Jung was also pleased to be in Zurich after living nearly all of his life in Basel, a city that he regarded as stuffy. Zurich, by contrast, was the beautiful city on the lovely lake surrounded by the Alps he had dreamed of as a boy. He was to remain here the rest of his life. The garden of his house in Kusnacht, a suburb of Zurich, fronted on the lake. Later he was to build a retreat at the far end of the lake.

In order to familiarize himself with his chosen speciality he isolated himself in the hospital for six months, observing patients and reading extensively in the psychiatric literature. "Dominating my interests and research was the burning question: 'What actually takes place inside the mentally ill?' " (MDR, p. 114). Not only did he learn from Bleuler but he spent several months in 1902 studying in Paris with the great French psychiatrist Pierre Janet.

But it was Sigmund Freud who was to have the greatest influence on Jung's thinking. He was familiar with Freud and Breuer's studies of hysteria, published in the 1890's, and he read Freud's *The Interpretation of Dreams* when it appeared in 1900. He said of this book that it was "a fount of illumination" for young psychiatrists.

Jung married Emma Rauschenbach in 1903, and she collaborated with him in his work until her death in 1955.

In 1905, at the age of thirty, Jung became lecturer in

psychiatry at the University of Zurich and senior physician at the Psychiatric Clinic. He also conducted a private practice, which soon grew so large that he had to resign the Clinic appointment. He continued to lecture on psychopathology, Freudian psychoanalysis, and the psychology of primitive people at the university until 1913.

While Jung was still associated with the clinic he established a research laboratory to investigate the psychic reactions of mental patients. For these investigations he used the word-association test in conjunction with physiological expressions of emotions. The word-association test consists of presenting a list of words, one at a time, to a person who has been instructed to respond with the first word he can think of. If the person hesitates unduly long before responding or if he expresses emotion, this indicates that the word has struck what Jung called a *complex* in the person. These investigations of complexes, some of which were published in American scientific journals, were responsible for establishing his reputation in the United States. As a result, he was invited to lecture on the word-association test studies at Clark University in Massachusetts in 1909. This was the first of many visits to the United States, a country of which he was very fond.

Meanwhile, Jung had been following Freud's writings closely and sent him copies of his articles and his first book, *The Psychology of Dementia Praecox* (1907), in which he upheld the Freudian viewpoint although with some reservations, especially concerning the importance of infantile sexual traumas. Freud invited Jung to visit him in Vienna in 1907. The two men were greatly attracted to each other, and they talked continuously for thirteen hours! Thus began a personal and professional relationship that was to last for six years. They corresponded on a weekly basis, and in 1909 both men received invitations to speak at Clark University and traveled together for seven weeks. In 1912 Jung returned to the United States to lecture at Fordham University on the theory of psychoanalysis. When the International Psychoanalytic Association was founded, Jung, at the insistence of Freud, became its first president. In a letter to Jung written about this time, Freud called him his adopted eldest son, his crown prince and successor.

It is not our intention to examine the reasons why the

relationship between these two titans of twentieth-century psychology and psychiatry was severed. Doubtless the causes were complex and "overdetermined." Suffice it to say that Jung was and always had been from childhood a very independent and self-sufficient person, and he could not have relished being anyone's disciple, eldest son, or "crown prince." He wanted to pursue his own line of thought, and did so in a book, *Symbols of Transformation,* which he was sure would cost him Freud's friendship as it did. For several months Jung was so tormented by this thought that he could not complete the final chapter, which was called "The Sacrifice." Sacrifice it was.

After the association with Freud and psychoanalysis was terminated, Jung described himself as being in a state of confusion and inner uncertainty. He resigned his lectureship at the university because he felt it was not fair for him to be teaching students when his own intellectual situation was disoriented. There followed a "fallow period" when Jung could do no research, reading, or writing. During this period he devoted his time to exploring his own unconscious by analyzing his dreams and visions.

After three years of dormancy, Jung again became intellectually active and wrote one of his finest books, *Psychological Types.* In this volume, published in 1921, Jung not only discussed his differences with Freud and with Adler, another psychoanalyst who broke with Freud, but more importantly he described a taxonomy of character types, including the famous distinctions between extraversion and introversion, and thinking and feeling.

About this time he began to have regular meetings with students in his home, and he began to travel more extensively. He went to Tunis and the Sahara Desert. He had always been interested in the mentality of primitive people, and he was now able to observe them firsthand. Although unfamiliar with the native language of the people, he observed their gestures, mannerisms, facial expressions, and emotional reactions. He felt considerably enriched and enlightened by this first African experience. Before the next trip to Africa he learned Swahili. He penetrated to the heart of Africa on a safari, returning by way of Egypt. This journey was a profound learning experience for Jung because it brought him in contact with primitive mentality and the collective unconscious. Memories of this trip never faded from his mind, and he referred to it again and again in his writings.

Jung traveled to New Mexico to learn about the Pueblo Indians' religious beliefs, which they concealed with utmost secrecy. Direct inquiry proved fruitless, so Jung used an indirect approach. He talked on various subjects and watched for emotional reactions. When their faces registered emotion, Jung knew he had touched a significant subject. It was an adaptation of the word-association method.

Jung had always been interested in Eastern religion and mythology, and trips to India and Ceylon reinforced his interest and broadened his knowledge. He wrote a great deal about the differences between the Eastern and Western personalities as expressed through their contrasting customs, religious beliefs and practices, and myths. He pointed out that the Eastern mind is typically introverted whereas the Western mind is predominantly extraverted.

Through his friendship with Richard Wilhelm, an authority on Chinese culture, Jung became familiar with the *I Ching,* an ancient text which describes a system of divination or fortunetelling. Wilhelm was also responsible for introducing Jung to alchemy, a subject Jung devoted himself to with great passion for many years, becoming an outstanding authority on this unusual topic. His book *Psychology and Alchemy,* published in 1944, is among his most important writings.

Jung has often been criticized for the interest he took in such scientifically suspect subjects as alchemy, astrology, divination, telepathy and clairvoyance, yoga, spiritualism, mediums and séances, fortunetelling, flying saucers, religious symbolism, visions, and dreams. In our opinion, these criticisms are not justified. Jung approached these subjects not as a disciple or a "believer," but as a psychologist. The central question for him was what these subjects revealed about the mind, especially that level of the mind which Jung called the collective unconscious. Jung learned very early in his career that the unconscious mind shows itself most clearly in the symptoms, verbalizations, hallucinations, and visions of patients such as those at Burghölzli. Later he was to discover that in more normal people, the unconscious manifested itself most clearly in so-called occult phenomena, religious symbolism, mythology, astrology, and dreams. As a student of the unconscious, Jung made use of whatever sources there were, no matter how outrageous they might be to other scientists. In this, as in so many other ways, Jung did not abide by convention and tradition. Nevertheless, he remained a scientist in his treatment of these subjects.

In his autobiography, Jung is reticent concerning his home life with his wife, four daughters, and son. Unlike many recent autobiographers, he makes no mention of his sexual feelings or behavior. He does say that it was essential for him to have a normal home life as a counterbalance for his strange inner world of dreams, fantasies, and occult experiences. "My family and my profession remained the base to which I could always return, assuring me that I was an actually existing, ordinary person" (MDR, p. 189). Jung saw his many patients, many of whom were well-known and accomplished people from all over the world, in his beautiful lakefront home in Kusnacht.

In 1922 Jung purchased property at the end of Lake Zurich in the village of Bollingen, and built a summer house. The first unit was circular in shape, resembling the style of an African dwelling, with a fireplace in the middle of the room and cots arranged around the wall. This arrangement proved to be too primitive, so a conventional two-story house was added to it. The circular tower became Jung's private retreat. The Jung family enjoyed the Bollingen place at every possible opportunity. Here they could go sailing, plant gardens, and enjoy the beauties of nature. It is to be noted that every place where Jung lived from the day he was born was on either a river or a lake.

Early in 1944 Jung broke his foot, and this accident was immediately followed by a heart attack. Following his recovery, he embarked on a very productive period of writing. He attributed this prolific period to the numerous visions, dreams, and deliriums he experienced during the months of recovery. The months in bed also provided time for organizing his thoughts and concepts.

After Jung's wife died in 1955, the pleasurable trips to the Bollingen retreat became more and more infrequent.

Although Jung employed a gardener and housekeeper, his daughters took turns staying with him in Kusnacht to keep him company. Jung's devoted secretary, Aniela Jaffé, also appeared daily to help with the large correspondence he had with people all over the world. Miss Jaffé was indispensable to Jung and remained with him until his death on June 6, 1961.

As would be expected of a man of Jung's intellectual stature, he was the recipient of many honors and tributes. He was awarded honorary degrees by a number of universities, including Harvard and Oxford. He was generous with his time, granting interviews, appearing before the camera and on television, giving talks and writing popular articles, answering letters, and receiving people from all over the world who came to visit him. He spoke freely and unaffectedly with everyone, famous people as well as high school students. He was an extremely democratic person without the slightest trace of snobbery or self-importance.

Since his death in 1961 Jung's influence has been steadily increasing. More people are reading his books today than ever before. His complete writings, consisting of nineteen volumes, are now available in English translation, and many of his works have been published in inexpensive paperbound editions. As yet there is no definitive biography of Jung.

Jung's concepts and methods of treatment are disseminated by training institutes located in cities around the world. The mecca of analytical psychology is still Zurich, where the C. G. Jung Institute, founded in 1948, is located. Students from many countries study at this institute under its distinguished faculty. C. A. Meier, who is regarded as Jung's successor, is professor at the famous Zurich Technological School and has his own clinic and research laboratory. There are an International Analytical Psychology Association as well as national and regional organizations which promulgate analytical psychology. Although Jungian psychology has not been taken up by universities to the same extent that Freudian psychology has, there are indications that academic psychologists in the United States are beginning to pay more attention to Jung. University students are definitely interested in Jung, and his books are widely read by them.

Jung himself was reluctant to make any comprehensive systematic formulation of his concepts, preferring to accumulate new observations and to obtain new insights rather than to summarize old ones. Again and again he asserted that he wanted to know and to understand the facts; theories for him were merely tentative conjectures or guesses, and they had to give way when they were contradicted by the hard facts of reality.

In reading the following chapters, the reader should bear in mind that the concepts described developed out of innumerable observations of the behavior of many individuals in the full and frank intimacy of the therapeutic situation. In addition to these consulting-room observations, Jung also drew upon what he learned from his travels, and from his vast knowledge of mythology, religion, alchemy, social phenomena, and occult subjects. Not to be ignored is his own self-analysis, which he engaged in throughout his life. We have seen what an introspective person he was, even as a child.

Another matter should be brought to the reader's attention. Scientific concepts are generalizations about reality that have been abstracted from many concrete observations. They are useful for calling attention to aspects of personality and behavior that all people share. How each of these abstract concepts functions in a specific individual's personality and behavior is what primarily interested Jung. He was always more drawn to the rich and puzzling complexity of the individual case—the person who sat before him in his consulting room—than to the abstract concepts, laws, and theories of science, necessary though he knew them to be. Jung was a well-trained scientist, but he was also a humanist. His interest in and concern for people was not subordinated to his role as a scientist. That is one reason why people in all walks of life were drawn to him.

III. WHAT WAS JUNG?

What sort of man was Jung? Physically he was tall, broad-shouldered, and strong. He was a mountain climber and expert sailor. He enjoyed gardening, splitting wood, chiseling stone, building, and other manual activities. He liked to play games. He was a good eater, drank wine, and smoked cigars and a pipe. He was an active, vigorous, healthy man.

Everyone who came into personal contact with Jung has commented on his joviality, the twinkle in his eyes, his hearty, infectious laugh, and his wonderful sense of humor. He was a good listener as well as an interesting talker, and he never appeared to be hurried or preoccupied. In conversation he was tolerant of different points of view, flexible in his approach to questions, and simple in speech. He preferred vernacular speech and was fond of interspersing his conversation, when talking with Americans, with American slang expressions. People felt comfortable in his presence.

Who was Jung? He was educated as a medical doctor, although he never had a general medical practice. Instead, he became a psychiatrist, first in a mental hospital and clinic, and then as a private practitioner. He was also a university professor. For a number of years he was closely identified with the Freudian school of psychoanalysis. After his break with Freud, he developed his own system of psychoanalysis. At first he called it *complex psychology,* and later *analytical psychology.* The system included not only a body of concepts and theoretical formulations, but also methods for treating people with psychological problems. Jung did not restrict his professional activities to the consulting room. He also applied his ideas by making a critical analysis of a vast array of social problems, religious issues, and trends in modern art. He was a scholar of impressive erudition, and read English, French, Latin, and Greek fluently as well as his native German. He was a writer of great talent. The city of Zurich awarded him its literary prize in 1932. He was a devoted husband and father, and an informed Swiss citizen. He belonged to the "Freethinking" or Democratic party.

Physician, psychiatrist, psychoanalyst, professor, scholar, writer, social critic, family man, and citizen—Jung was all of these. First and foremost, however, he was a relentless student of the psyche. That is, he was a psychologist. It is as a psychologist that he would like to be remembered, and will be.

He said, ". . . the sole purpose of human existence is to kindle a light in the darkness of mere being."

REFERENCE

JUNG, C. G. *Memories, Dreams, Reflections.* New York: Vintage Books, 1961.

CHAPTER TWO

The Structure of Personality

A complete conception of human personality attempts to give answers to three sets of questions. What are the constituents that make up the structure of personality, and how do these components interact with one another and with the external world? What are the sources of energy that activate the personality and how is the energy distributed among the various components? How does the personality originate and what changes take place in it throughout the life of the individual? These three sets of questions may be called *structural*, *dynamic*, and *developmental*, respectively.

Because Jungian psychology tries to give answers to all of these questions, it may be regarded as a comprehensive theory of personality. In this chapter, we will discuss the concepts put forth by Jung to describe the structure of personality.

Before doing this, let us say a few words about the nature of scientific concepts. A concept is a descriptive name or tag for a group of observed facts about some natural phenomenon together with the ideas, inferences, or hypotheses that attempt to account for the observed facts. A concept, therefore, is a general or abstract term. For example, the word *evolution* as conceived by Darwin refers to a complex set of observations and explanations regarding the origin of species. In order to understand a concept one must have some knowledge of the observations upon which it is based. This means that in discussing a concept one must go from the general to the particulars, which is the reverse of what the scientist did in formulating the concept. This is what we will do in describing Jung's concepts. We will first discuss a concept in general terms and then give concrete examples of it.

The most useful concepts are those that can be applied widely. Jungian concepts possess this feature; they are very broad in their scope. Because of their breadth we cannot possibly discuss all the possible applications and ramifications they may have. The reader is encouraged to think of other manifestations of the concept in addition to the examples we present. He should find his knowledge of personality and individuality greatly enhanced by seeing how the concepts express themselves in his own personality and in the behavior of people known to him.

Concepts have their dangers, too, as Jung realized. A concept may bias or limit our observations so that we see things that *do not* exist or we do not see things that *do* exist. That is why Jung cautioned against becoming too attached to one's concepts and why he insisted upon the priority of observable facts over theories.

I. THE PSYCHE

In Jungian psychology the personality as a whole is called the *psyche*. This Latin word originally meant "spirit" or "soul," but in modern times it has come to mean "mind," as in *psychology*, the science of mind. The psyche embraces all thought, feeling, and behavior, both conscious and unconscious. It functions as a guide which regulates and adapts the individual to his social and physical environment. "Psychology is neither biology nor physiology nor any other science than just this knowledge of the psyche" (*Collected Works*, Vol. 9i, p. 30).

The concept of the psyche affirms Jung's primary idea that a person is a whole to begin with. He is not an assemblage of parts, each of which has been added through experience and learning much as one might furnish a house piece by piece. This concept of the original wholeness of personality may seem obvious and trite were it not for the fact that many psychological theories state or imply that man's personality is acquired part by part, and that only later, if at all, does any sort of coherent organized unity appear. Jung explicitly rejects this jigsaw conception of personality. Man does not strive for wholeness; he already has it, he is born with it. What he must do throughout his life span, Jung says, is to develop this inherent wholeness to the greatest degree of differentiation, coherence, and harmony possible, and to guard against it breaking up into separate, autonomous, and conflicting systems. A dissociated personality is a deformed personality. Jung's work as a psychoanalyst was to help patients recover their lost wholeness, and to strengthen the psyche so it could resist future dismemberment. Thus, for Jung, the ultimate goal of psychoanalysis is psychosynthesis.

The psyche is composed of numerous diversified but interacting systems and levels. Three levels in the psyche can be distinguished. These are *consciousness*, the *personal unconscious*, and the *collective unconscious*.

II. CONSCIOUSNESS

Consciousness is the only part of the mind that is known directly by the individual. It appears early in life, probably prior to birth. When observing a young child one can observe conscious awareness operating as the child recognizes and identifies his parents, his toys, and other objects in his surroundings. His conscious awareness grows daily through the application of the four mental functions that Jung called *thinking, feeling, sensing,* and *intuiting.* The child does not use all four of these functions in equal proportions; he will usually utilize one function considerably more than he uses the others. The predominant use of one of these four functions is what differentiates one child's basic character from that of another child. For instance, if a child is predominantly a *thinking* type, his character will differ significantly from the character of a child who is predominantly a *feeling* type.

In addition to the four mental functions, there are two attitudes that determine the orientation of the conscious mind. These attitudes are *extraversion* and *introversion.* The extraverted attitude orients consciousness toward the external, objective world; the introverted attitude orients consciousness toward the inner, subjective world. (We shall have more to say about these functions and attitudes in Chapter Five.)

The process by which the consciousness of a person becomes individualized or differentiated from other people is known as individuation. Individuation plays a major role in psychological development. (See Chapter Four.) Jung wrote, "I use the term 'individuation' to denote the process by which a person becomes a psychological 'in-dividual,' that is, a separate, indivisible unity or 'whole' " (Vol. 9i, p. 275).

The goal of individuation is knowing oneself as completely as possible, or self-consciousness. In modern terminology it would be called expanding consciousness. "In the final analysis," Jung wrote, "the decisive factor is always consciousness" (MDR, p. 187). Individuation and consciousness go hand in hand in the development of a personality; the beginning of consciousness is also the beginning of individuation. With increasing consciousness, there is also greater individuation. A person who remains oblivious of himself and of the world around him cannot be a very individuated person. From the process of the individuation of consciousness a new element is produced which Jung called the *ego*.

A. THE EGO   The ego is the name Jung uses for the organization of the conscious mind; it is composed of conscious perceptions, memories, thoughts, and feelings. Although the ego occupies a small portion of the total psyche, it plays the vitally important function of gatekeeper to consciousness. Unless the ego acknowledges the presence of an idea, a feeling, a memory, or a perception, it cannot be brought into awareness. The ego is highly selective. It resembles a distillery; much psychic material is fed into it but little comes out or reaches the level of full awareness. Every day we are subjected to a vast number of experiences, most of which do not become conscious because the ego eliminates them before they reach consciousness. This is an important function, for otherwise we would be overwhelmed by the mass of material that would crowd into consciousness.

The ego provides identity and continuity for a personality because by the selection and elimination of psychic material the ego can maintain a continuous quality of coherence in the individual personality. It is because of the ego that we feel ourselves to be the same person today that we were yesterday. In this respect, individuation and the ego work in close relationship to each other in developing a distinctive and ongoing personality. The person can become individuated only to the extent that the ego permits incoming experiences to become conscious.

What determines what the ego will allow to become conscious and what it will reject? Partly it is determined by the dominant function. If a person is a feeling type, the ego will permit more emotional experiences to enter consciousness. If he is a thinking type, thoughts will be admitted into consciousness more readily than feelings. Partly it is due to the amount of anxiety that the experience arouses in the ego. Ideas and memories that evoke anxiety are apt to be refused admittance to awareness (consciousness). Partly it is due to the level of individuation reached. The ego of a highly individuated person will allow more things to become conscious. And partly it is due to the intensity of the experience. Very strong experiences can batter their way through the gates of the ego, whereas weak ones are easily repelled.

III. THE PERSONAL UNCONSCIOUS

What happens to experiences that fail to gain recognition by the ego? They do not disappear from the psyche, for nothing that has been experienced ceases to exist. Instead they are stored in what Jung called the *personal unconscious*. This level of the mind adjoins the ego. It is the receptacle that contains all those psychic activities and contents which are incongruous with the conscious individuation or function. Or, they were once conscious experiences which have been repressed or disregarded for various reasons, such as a distressing thought, an unsolved problem, a personal conflict, or a moral issue. Often they are forgotten simply because they were irrelevant or seemed unimportant at the time they were experienced. All experiences that are too weak to reach consciousness, or too weak to remain in consciousness, are stored in the personal unconscious.

The contents of the personal unconscious are ordinarily readily accessible to consciousness when the need for them arises. Some examples may make this two-way traffic between the personal unconscious and the ego clearer. A person knows the names of a number of friends and acquaintances. Naturally, they do not remain in consciousness all of the time, but they are available when needed. Where are they when they are not in consciousness? They are in the personal unconscious, which is like an elaborate filing system or memory bank. Another example. We may learn or observe something that is of little or no interest to us at the time. Years later it may become highly relevant and then is summoned forth from the personal unconscious. Experiences that have passed unnoticed during the day may appear in a dream that night. As a matter of fact, the personal unconscious plays an important part in the production of dreams.

A. COMPLEXES   One interesting and important feature of the personal unconscious is that groups of contents may clump together to form a cluster or constellation. Jung called them *complexes*. The first intimation of the existence of complexes was obtained in Jung's studies using the word-association test. It will be recalled from our discussion of this test in the preceding chapter that a list of words is read off one at a time and the person is instructed to respond with the first word that comes into his mind. Jung observed that sometimes the person would take a long time to make a response. When he asked him why it took him so long to reply, the person could not explain the delay. Jung guessed that the delay was caused by an unconscious emotion that inhibited the response. When he explored this matter further he found that other words which were related to the one that had evoked a delay also produced long reaction times. He then reasoned that there must be associated groups of feelings, thoughts, and memories (complexes) in the unconscious. Any word that touched upon this complex would cause a delayed response. Further study of these complexes indicated that they are like separate little personalities within the total personality. They are autonomous, possess their own driving force, and can be very powerful in controlling our thoughts and behavior.

It is due to Jung that the word *complex* has become a part of our everyday language. We speak of a person as having an inferiority complex or a complex about sex or money or "the younger generation" or about almost anything. Everyone is familiar with the Oedipus complex described by Freud. When we say a person has a complex we mean he is so strongly preoccupied by something that he can hardly think about anything else. In modern parlance, he has a "hangup." A strong complex is easily noticed by others, although the person himself may not be aware of it.

An example described by Jung is the *mother complex.* The person who is dominated by a strong mother complex is extremely sensitive to everything his mother says and feels, and the image of her is always foremost in his mind. He will try to introduce his mother or something associated with her into every possible conversation whether it is pertinent or not. He will favor stories, movies, and events in which mothers play a prominent role. He looks forward to Mother's Day and his mother's birthday or any other occasion on which he can honor her. He will tend to imitate his mother by assuming her preferences and interests, and he will be attracted to her friends. He prefers the company of older women to women his own age. As a child, he is a "mother's boy"; as an adult he is still "tied to his mother's apron strings."

Most of the complexes Jung observed were those of his patients, and he recognized that complexes were deeply implicated in their neurotic condition. "A person does not have a complex; the complex has him." An aim of analytical therapy is to dissolve complexes and to free the person from their tyranny over his life.

But a complex, as Jung was to discover, need not be a hindrance to a person's adjustment. In fact, quite the contrary. They can be and often are sources of inspiration and drive which are essential for outstanding achievement. For example, an artist obsessed with beauty will settle for no less than a masterpiece. He will produce numerous works of art, improving his technique and deepening his consciousness in an effort to produce something of sublime beauty. One thinks of Van Gogh, who gave the last years of his life to art. He was like a man possessed, and he sacrificed everything, including his health and finally his life, to painting. Jung speaks of the artist's "ruthless passion for creation." "He is fated to sacrifice happiness and everything that makes life worth living for the ordinary human being" (Vol. 15, pp. 101-102). This striving for perfection must be credited to a *strong* complex; a *weak* complex would restrict one to producing mediocre or inferior works, or none at all.

How do complexes originate? At first, under the influence of Freud, Jung was inclined to believe they had their origin in traumatic experiences in early childhood. For example, a child might be abruptly separated from his mother, which could give rise to an enduring mother complex as a compensation for the lost mother. Jung was not to be satisfied with this explanation for very long. He came to the realization that complexes must originate out of something much deeper in human nature than early childhood experiences. Prompted by curiosity over what this deeper something might be, Jung discovered another level of the psyche, which he called the *collective unconscious*.

IV. THE COLLECTIVE UNCONSCIOUS

Jung's analysis of complexes was of major importance and was responsible for bringing his name to the attention of the scientific world of psychology and psychiatry while he was still a relatively young man. He was only thirty-three when he was invited to lecture at Clark University in Massachusetts. Important as the discovery of the complex was, his discovery of the collective unconscious was of far greater significance and made him one of the outstanding intellects of this century. It also made him a very controversial figure.

The reason for the importance of the concept of a collective unconscious is as follows. The ego as the center of consciousness and the personal unconscious as a storehouse of repressed psychic material were not new concepts. Psychologists had been studying consciousness since the 1860's, when scientific psychology emerged as a discipline independent of philosophy and physiology. The study of the unconscious mind had been initiated by Freud in the 1890's, and his work was well known to Jung.

Both the conscious mind and the unconscious mind were seen, for the most part, as originating out of experience. Repression of traumatic childhood experiences formed the unconscious, according to Freud, although he was to modify this view later, possibly as a consequence of Jung's influence. In any event, it was Jung who broke free from a strictly environmental determinism of the mind, and showed that evolution and heredity provide the blueprints of the psyche just as they provide the blueprints of the body. The discovery of the collective unconscious was a landmark in the history of psychology.

The mind, through its physical counterpart, the brain, has inherited characteristics that determine the ways in which a person will react to life's experiences and even determine what type of experiences he will have. The mind of man is prefigured by evolution. Thus, the individual is linked with his past, not only with the past of his infancy but more importantly with the past of the species and before that with the long stretch of organic evolution. This placing of the psyche within the evolutionary process was Jung's preeminent achievement.

Let us proceed to delineate the characteristics and contents of the collective unconscious. First of all, it is that portion of the psyche which can be differentiated from the personal unconscious by the fact that its existence is not dependent upon personal experience. The personal unconscious is composed of contents that were once conscious, but the contents of the collective unconscious have never been conscious, within the lifetime of the individual.

The collective unconscious is a reservoir of latent images, usually called *primordial images* by Jung. *Primordial* means "first" or "original"; therefore a primordial image refers to the earliest development of the psyche. Man inherits these images from his ancestral past, a past that includes all of his human ancestors as well as his prehuman or animal ancestors. These racial images are not inherited in the sense that a person consciously remembers or has images that his ancestors had. Rather they are predispositions or potentialities for experiencing and responding to the world in the same ways that his ancestors did. Consider, for example, man's fear of snakes or of the dark. He does not have to learn these fears through experiences with snakes or the dark, although such experiences may reinforce or reaffirm his predispositions. We inherit predispositions to fear snakes and the dark because our primitive ancestors experienced these fears for countless generations. They became engraved upon the brain.

Perhaps this is the place to discuss a criticism that has often been made of Jung's explanation of the origin of the collective unconscious. Two views of the mechanism of evolution have been put forward by biologists. One view states that what is learned through experience by previous generations can be inherited by future generations, and does not need to be learned by them anew. Habits become instincts. This is called the doctrine of acquired characters, or Lamarckism after its founder. The other view of the mechanism of evolution, and one that is accepted by most biologists, is that evolution proceeds by changes (called mutations) in the germ plasm. Mutations which favor the adaptation of the individual to his environment, and which increase his chances of survival and of reproduction, tend to be passed along from generation to generation. Mutations which disfavor adaptation, survival, and reproduction are eliminated.

Jung, unfortunately, adopted the unpopular Lamarckian explanation: Fear of snakes or of the dark learned by one generation or a sequence of generations can be inherited by succeeding generations. It should be pointed out, however, that the concept of a collective unconscious does not require an explanation in terms of acquired characteristics. The collective unconscious can also be explained by mutation and natural selection. That is, a mutation or a series of mutations can result in a predisposition to fear snakes. Since primitive man was exposed to harm from poisonous snakes, his fear of them would cause him to take precautions against being bitten. Thus, the mutation or mutations that caused the fear and hence the precautions would increase man's chances of survival so that the changes in the germ plasm would be passed on to succeeding generations. In other words, the evolution of a collective unconscious can be accounted for in the same way that the evolution of the body is explained. Because the brain is the principal organ of the mind, the collective unconscious depends directly upon the evolution of the brain.

After that necessary digression, let us return to a description of the collective unconscious. Man is born with many predispositions for thinking, feeling, perceiving, and acting in specific ways. The development and expression of these predispositions or latent images depend *entirely* upon the individual's experiences. As already mentioned, a fear of something can develop quite easily if the predisposition to feel fear already exists in the collective unconscious. Very little stimulation is necessary in some cases in order for the predisposition to manifest itself. The first time we see a snake, even a harmless one, we may be terrified. In other cases, the predisposition may require considerable stimulation from the environment before it emerges from the collective unconscious.

The contents of the collective unconscious exercise a preformed pattern for personal behavior to follow from the day the individual is born. "The form of the world into which he is born is already inborn in him as a virtual image" (Vol. 7, p. 188). This virtual image comes into conscious reality by identifying itself with corresponding objects in the world. For example, if a virtual image of the mother exists in the collective unconscious it will quickly express itself by the infant's perceiving and reacting to its actual mother. Thus, the contents of the collective unconscious are responsible for the selectivity of perception and action. We easily perceive some things and react to them in certain ways because the collective unconscious is predisposed to them.

The more experiences we have, the greater are the chances that the latent images will become manifested. That is why a rich environment and opportunities for education and learning are necessary for individuating (making conscious) all aspects of the collective unconscious.

A. ARCHETYPES The contents of the collective unconscious are called *archetypes*. The word archetype means an original model after which other similar things are patterned. A synonym is *prototype*.

Jung spent much time during the last forty years of his life investigating and writing about the archetypes. Among the numerous archetypes that he identified and described are those of birth, rebirth, death, power, magic, the hero, the child, the trickster, God, the demon, the wise old man, the earth mother, the giant, many natural objects like trees, the sun, the moon, wind, rivers, fire, and animals, and many man-made objects such as rings and weapons. Jung wrote, "There are as many archetypes as there are typical situations in life. Endless repetition has engraved these experiences into our psychic constitution, not in the forms of images filled with content, but at first only as *forms without content,* representing merely the possibility of a certain type of perception and action" (Vol. 9i, p. 48).

It is very important for a correct understanding of Jung's theory of archetypes that archetypes are not to be regarded as fully developed pictures in the mind like memory images of past experiences in one's life. The mother archetype, for example, is not a photograph of a mother or a woman. It is more like a negative that has to be developed by experience. Jung wrote, "A primordial image is determined as to its content only when it becomes conscious and is therefore filled out with the material of conscious experience" (Vol. 9i, p. 79).

Some archetypes are of such great importance in shaping our personality and behavior that Jung devoted special attention to them. These are the *persona,* the *anima* and *animus,* the *shadow,* and the *self.* They will be described below.

Although archetypes are separate structures in the collective unconscious they can form combinations. For example, if the hero archetype combines with the demon archetype, the result could be a "ruthless leader" type of person. Or if the magic and birth archetypes blend together, the result could be a "fertility magician" found in some primitive cultures. These magicians perform fertility rites for young brides to ensure that they will have children. Since the archetypes are capable of interacting with each other in various combinations, this also becomes a factor in producing personality differences among individuals.

Archetypes are universal: that is, everyone inherits the same basic archetypal images. Every infant throughout the world inherits a mother archetype. This preformed image of the mother is then developed into a definite image by the actual mother's appearance and behavior and by the relationships and experiences the baby has with her. Individual differences in the expression of the mother archetype soon appear, however, since experiences with mothers and child-rearing practices vary from family to family and even between one child and another in the same family. Jung does note, however, that when racial differentiation took place, essential differences in the collective unconscious of the various races also appeared.

In our previous discussion concerning complexes, we suggested several possible origins for them. The archetype must now be included in that list, for it is, in fact, the nucleus of a complex. The archetype, acting as a center or nucleus, functions as a magnet, attracting relevant experiences to it to form a complex. After gaining sufficient strength from the addition of experiences, the complex can penetrate into consciousness. It is only by being the center of a well-developed complex that the archetype can find expression in consciousness and behavior.

Consider, for example, the development of a *God* complex out of the God archetype. This archetype, like all other archetypes, exists first in the collective unconscious. As the person experiences the world, those experiences that are relevant to the God archetype become attached to it to form the complex. The complex becomes stronger and stronger by virtue of the accumulation of new material until it is strong enough to force its way into consciousness. If the God complex becomes dominant, then much of what the person experiences and how he behaves is governed by the God complex. He perceives and judges everything in terms of good and evil, he preaches hellfire and damnation for the wicked and eternal paradise for the virtuous, he accuses people of living in sin and demands repentance from them. He believes himself to be God's prophet or even God himself, and that only he can reveal the paths of righteousness and salvation to mankind. Such a man would be considered a fanatic or psychotic. His complex has seized control of his entire personality. This example is one of a complex operating in an extreme and unlimited capacity. If this man's God complex had functioned as a *portion* of his personality instead of taking over his *total* personality, he might have been of great service to humanity.

Let us now consider the four archetypes that play such important roles in everyone's personality.

1. *The Persona* The word *persona* originally denoted a mask worn by an actor which enabled him to portray a specific role in a play. (Other words derived from the same source are *person* and *personality*.) In Jungian psychology, the persona archetype serves a similar purpose; it enables one to portray a character that is not necessarily his own. The persona is the mask or facade one exhibits publicly, with the intention of presenting a favorable impression so that society will accept him. It might also be called the *conformity* archetype.

All archetypes must be advantageous to the individual and to the race; otherwise they would not have become a part of man's inherent nature. The persona is necessary for survival. It enables us to get along with people, even those we dislike, in an amicable manner. It can lead to personal gain and achievement. It is the basis for social and community life. Consider, for example, a young man who gets a job with a large corporation. In order to get ahead he must find out what role is expected of him. This will probably include personal characteristics such as grooming, clothing, and manners. It is sure to include relations with his superiors, and perhaps his political opinions, the neighborhood he lives in, the kind of car he drives, his wife, and a number of other things deemed important for the corporate image. If, as the saying goes, he plays his cards right he will win the game. Of course, he must perform his work well, be industrious, diligent, responsible, and dependable. But these qualities, too, are part of the persona. A young man or woman who cannot wear the mask of the corporate image inevitably finds himself passed over for advancement or out of a job.

Another advantage of the persona is that the material rewards it brings can be used to lead a more satisfying, and perhaps a more natural, private life. The employee who wears the corporate mask eight hours a day can take it off when he leaves the office and engage in activities that are more fulfilling to him. One is reminded in this connection of Franz Kafka, the eminent writer, who worked conscientiously for a state insurance office during the day and spent his evenings writing and pursuing cultural activities. He confessed repeatedly that he hated his work, but his superiors would never have guessed this feeling from the way he applied himself to the requirements of the job. Many people lead dual lives, one which is dominated by the persona, and one which satisfies other psychic needs.

A person may have more than one mask. At home he may wear a different mask than he wears at work. He may put on a third mask when he goes out to play golf or poker with his friends. Collectively, however, all of his masks constitute his persona. He merely conforms in different ways in different situations. Of course, conformity has always been recognized as an important factor in social life, but no one before Jung suggested that it was the expression of an inborn archetype.

The role of the persona in the personality can be harmful as well as beneficial. If a person becomes too involved and too preoccupied with the role he is playing, and his ego begins to identify solely with this role, the other sides of his personality will be shoved aside. Such a persona-ridden person becomes alienated from his nature, and lives in a state of tension because of the conflict between his overdeveloped persona and the underdeveloped parts of the personality. The ego's identification with the persona is called *inflation*. On the one hand, the person has an exaggerated sense of self-importance which derives from playing a role so successfully. He is "putting it over" on people. Often he tries to project this role on others and demands that they play the same role. If he is in a position of authority, he can make life miserable for those who are in his power. Parents sometimes try to project their personas on their children, with unfortunate consequences. Customs and laws that relate to personal conduct are an expression of a group persona. They attempt to impose uniform standards of behavior on the whole group without regard to the needs of the individual. The hazards to mental health from inflation of the persona are self-evident.

On the other hand, the victim of inflation can also suffer feelings of inferiority and self-reproach when he is incapable of living up to the standards expected of him. He may as a result feel alienated from the community and experience feelings of loneliness and estrangement.

Jung had ample opportunity to study the effects of an inflated persona because so many of his patients were its victims. They were people, often of the greatest accomplishments, who suddenly realized their lives were empty and meaningless. In analysis they began to realize that they had been deceiving themselves for years, that they were hypocritical about their feelings and interests, and that they pretended to be interested in things which really did not interest them at all. Often they were people who had reached middle age before the crisis of the inflated persona came to a head. The aim of the treatment is, of course, self-evident. The persona has to be deflated in order to let the other sides of one's nature assert themselves. This is a difficult undertaking for a person who has been identifying with his persona for many years.

This discussion of an inflated persona suggests that it is better for one's psychic health to be a conscious hypocrite than an unconscious one, just as it is better to deceive others than to deceive oneself. Ideally, there should be no hypocrisy or no deception of any kind. For better or worse, however, the persona is a fact of human existence and must find expression, preferably in a modest form.

2. *The Anima and the Animus*   Jung called the persona the "outward face" of the psyche because it is that face which the world sees. The "inward face" he called the *anima* in males and the *animus* in females. The anima archetype is the feminine side of the male psyche; the animus archetype is the masculine side of the female psyche. Every person has qualities of the opposite sex, not only in the biological sense that man and woman secrete both male and female sex hormones but also in a psychological sense of attitudes and feelings.

Man has developed his anima archetype by continuous exposure to women over many generations, and woman has developed her animus archetype by her exposure to men. Through living and interacting with one another for generations, each sex has acquired characteristics of the opposite sex that facilitate appropriate responses and understanding of the opposite sex. Thus the anima and animus archetypes, like that of the persona, have strong survival value.

If the personality is to be well adjusted and harmoniously balanced, the feminine side of a man's personality and the masculine side of a woman's personality must be allowed to express themselves in consciousness and behavior. If a man exhibits only masculine traits, his feminine traits remain unconscious and therefore these traits remain undeveloped and primitive. This gives the unconscious a quality of weakness and impressionability. That is why the most virile-appearing and virile-acting man is often weak and submissive inside. A woman who exhibits excessive femininity in her external life would have the unconscious qualities of stubbornness or willfulness, qualities that are often present in man's outer behavior.

"Every man carries within him the eternal image of the woman, not the image of this or that particular woman, but a definite feminine image. This image is fundamentally unconscious, an hereditary factor of primordial origin engraved in the living organic system of the man, an imprint or archetype of all the ancestral experiences of the female, a deposit, as it were, of all the impressions ever made by woman ... Since this image is unconscious, it is always unconsciously projected upon the person of the beloved, and is one of the chief reasons for passionate attraction or aversion" (Vol. 17, p. 198).

What Jung is saying here is that man inherits his image of woman, and he unconsciously establishes certain standards that will strongly influence his acceptance or rejection of any specific woman. The first projection of the anima is always on the mother, just as the first projection of the animus is on the father. Later he projects it on those women who arouse his feelings in a positive or negative sense. If he experiences a "passionate attraction," the woman undoubtedly has the same traits as his anima-image of woman. Conversely, if he experiences "aversion," the woman would be one that possesses conflicting qualities to his unconscious anima-image. The same events take place for the woman's projection of her animus.

Although a man may have numerous reasons for being attracted to a woman, these reasons can only be secondary ones, for the primary reasons are set forth in the unconscious. Men have attempted numerous relationships with women that were contrary to their anima-image, which inevitably result in dissatisfaction and antagonism.

Jung says that the anima has a preconceived liking for everything that is vain, helpless, uncertain, and unintentional in a woman. The animus chooses to identify with men who are heroic, intellectual, artistic, or athletic celebrities.

We said earlier that many people suffer from inflated or overdeveloped personas. The opposite condition is more often true of the anima or animus. These archetypes are often deflated or underdeveloped. One reason for this difference is that Western civilization seems to place a high value on conformity and to disparage femininity in men and masculinity in women. The disparagement begins in childhood when "sissies" and "tomboys" are ridiculed. Boys are expected to conform to a culturally specified masculine role and girls to a feminine role. Thus, the persona takes precedence over and stifles the anima or animus.

One consequence of this imbalance between the persona and anima or animus is that it may trigger off a rebellion of the anima or animus, in which case the person over-reacts. A young man may accentuate his anima to the extent that he is more feminine than masculine. Some male transvestites and some effeminate homosexuals fall into this category. A man's identification with his anima may be so complete that he will undergo hormonal treatment and genital surgery to turn himself into a physically appearing woman. Or a young woman may identify so completely with her animus that she has her feminine features changed in order to appear more masculine.

3. *The Shadow* The anima or animus, as we have said, is projected on the opposite sex and is responsible for the quality of the relationships between the sexes. There is another archetype that represents one's own gender and that influences a person's relationships with his own sex. Jung called this archetype the *shadow*.

The shadow contains more of man's basic animal nature than any other archetype does. Because of its extremely deep roots in evolutionary history, it is probably the most powerful and potentially the most dangerous of all the archetypes. It is the source of all that is best and worst in man, especially in his relations with others of the same sex.

In order for a person to become an integral member of the community, it is necessary to tame his animal spirits contained in the shadow. This taming is accomplished by suppressing manifestations of the shadow and by developing a strong persona which counteracts the power of the shadow. The person who suppresses the animal side of his nature may become civilized, but he does so at the expense of decreasing the motive power for spontaneity, creativity, strong emotions, and deep insights. He cuts himself off from the wisdom of his instinctual nature, a wisdom that may be more profound than any learning or culture can provide. A shadowless life tends to become shallow and spiritless.

The shadow is persistent, however; it does not yield easily to suppression. This may be illustrated by the following example. A farmer may be inspired to be a poet. Inspirations are always the work of the shadow. The farmer does not think this inspiration is feasible at the time, probably because his persona as a farmer is too strong, so he rejects it. But the idea keeps plaguing him because of the persistent pressure exerted by the shadow. Each time it recurs he puts it aside. Finally, one day he gives in and turns from farming to writing poetry. Undoubtedly there were also secondary circumstances that promoted the decision, but the most powerful influence must be credited to the shadow for its persistence in reasserting the idea after it had been rejected several times. Even the secondary circumstances are primarily the work of the shadow building its foundation. The shadow in this respect is an important and valuable archetype because it has the capacity to retain and assert ideas or images that may turn out to be advantageous to the individual. By its tenacity it can thrust a person into more satisfying and creative activities.

When the ego and the shadow work in close harmony, the person feels full of life and vigor. The ego channels instead of obstructing the forces emanating from the instincts. Consciousness is expanded and there is a liveliness and vitality to mental activity. And not only mental activity; the person is also physically more alive and vigorous. It is not surprising, therefore, that creative people appear to be filled with animal spirits, so much so in some cases that more mundane people regard them to be freaks. There is some truth to the relationship between genius and madness. The shadow of the very creative person may overwhelm his ego from time to time, causing the person to appear temporarily insane.

Let us consider the fate of the "evil" or "nefarious" elements that exist in the shadow. A person might think that when the evil elements are eliminated from consciousness they are disposed of once and for all. This is not the case. They have simply withdrawn into the unconscious, where they will remain in a latent state as long as all is going well in the conscious ego. But if the person finds himself faced by a crisis or difficult life situation, the shadow will use this opportunity to exert its power over the ego. An example would be the compulsive alcoholic who succeeds in overcoming the habit. The reasons for him becoming an alcoholic in the first place would, when he is cured, be forced to reside in the unconscious, awaiting an opportunity to express themselves. This opportunity would become available if the person experiences a traumatic, adverse, or conflict-containing situation that he could not handle. The shadow then steps in with little resistance from the weakened ego, and the person reverts to alcoholism. The shadow has tremendous staying power; it never really surrenders. The persistent nature of the shadow is equally effective whether it is promoting something evil or something good.

When the shadow is stringently repressed by society or when inadequate outlets are provided for it, disaster often ensues. Writing in 1918 at the end of World War I, Jung observed that the "animal in us only becomes more beastlike" when it is repressed. He goes on to say that "that is no doubt the reason why no religion is so defiled with the spilling of innocent blood as Christianity, and why the world has never seen a bloodier war than the war of the Christian nations" (Vol. 10, p. 22). The implication of these observations is that Christian teachings are very repressive of the shadow. The same observation could be made regarding World War II, which was even bloodier, and the subsequent wars. In these cases, and innumerable others that might be cited from history, the repressed shadow strikes back, engulfing nations in wanton bloodshed.

We have said that the shadow is responsible for one's relations with the same sex. These relations may be either friendly or hostile depending upon whether the shadow is

accepted by the ego and becomes incorporated harmoniously into the psyche, or whether it is rejected by the ego
and banished to the unconscious. Men tend to project their
rejected shadow impulses on other men so that bad
feelings often arise between males. The same is true for
women.

As mentioned earlier, the shadow contains the basic or
normal instincts, and is the source of realistic insights and
appropriate responses that have survival value. These
qualities of the shadow are of great importance to the
individual in time of need. One is often faced by situations
that require immediate decisions and reactions; there is no
time to evaluate the situation and think about the most
suitable response. Under such circumstances, the conscious
mind (ego) becomes stunned by the sudden impact of the
situation, which allows the unconscious mind (shadow) to
deal with it in its own way. If the shadow has been
allowed to individuate, the reactions of the shadow to
threats and dangers may be very effective. But if the
shadow has been repressed and remains undifferentiated,
the surging forth of man's instinctive nature may further
overwhelm the ego and cause the person to collapse into
helplessness.

In summary, then, it may be said of the shadow
archetype that it gives to man's personality a full-bodied,
three-dimensional quality. These instincts are responsible
for man's vitality, creativity, vivacity, and vigor. Rejection of the shadow flattens the personality.

4. *The Self*   The concept of the total personality or psyche
is a central feature of Jung's psychology. This wholeness,
as pointed out in the discussion of the psyche, is not
achieved by putting the parts together in a jigsaw fashion;
it is there to begin with, although it takes time to mature.
The organizing principle of the personality is an archetype
which Jung called the *self*. The self is the central archetype in the collective unconscious, much as the sun is
the center of the solar system. The self is the archetype of
order, organization, and unification; it draws to itself and
harmonizes all the archetypes and their manifestations in
complexes and consciousness. It unites the personality,
giving it a sense of "oneness" and firmness. When a person
says he feels in harmony with himself and with the world,

we can be sure that the self archetype is performing its work effectively. On the other hand, when a person feels "out of sorts" and discontented, or more seriously conflicted and feels he is "going to pieces," the self is not doing its job properly.

The ultimate goal of every personality is to achieve a state of selfhood and self-realization. This is not a simple undertaking, but a very lengthy, difficult, and complicated task which is rarely, if ever, completely achieved by anyone. Great religious leaders like Jesus and Buddha come closest to having achieved it. As Jung points out, the self archetype does not even become evident until about middle age, since the personality must become fully developed through individuation before the self can become manifest with any degree of completeness. (See Chapter Four.)

Achieving a state of self-realization depends largely upon the cooperation of the ego; for if the ego ignores messages from the self archetype an appreciation and understanding of the self would be impossible. Everything must become conscious in order to have the effect of individuating the personality.

Knowledge of the self is accessible through the study of one's dreams. More importantly, through true religious experiences one can understand and realize the self. In Eastern religions the ritualistic practices for achieving selfhood, such as the meditation aspects of yoga, enable Eastern man to perceive the self more readily than Western man does. When Jung speaks of religion, he is referring to spiritual development and not to supernatural phenomena.

Jung counsels that less emphasis should be placed on obtaining total self-realization, and more emphasis should be placed on knowledge of one's self. Self-knowledge is the path to self-realization. This is an important distinction, because many people want to fulfill themselves without having the slightest knowledge of themselves. They want instant perfection, a miracle that will transform them into a fully realized person. Actually, the task is the most arduous one man faces in his life, requiring constant discipline, persistent efforts, and the highest responsibility and wisdom.

By making conscious that which is unconscious, man

can live in greater harmony with his own nature. He will experience fewer irritations and frustrations because he recognizes their origins in his own unconscious. A person who does not know his unconscious self projects the repressed elements of his unconscious on others. He accuses them of his own unrecognized faults, thus criticizing and condemning them, while all the time he is really projecting an unconscious part of himself. Self-awareness exposes these projections, and he is no longer compelled to seek victims to criticize and scorn. His relationships with people improve and he feels more in harmony with them and with himself.

The self archetype can be described as an inner guiding factor which is quite different from our outer conscious ego. The self has the capacity to regulate or govern, and influence the personality, enabling it to mature and increase its perceptiveness. Through development of the self man becomes motivated to increase his awareness, perception, understanding, and the direction of his life.

The concept of the self archetype is the most important result of Jung's investigations of the collective unconscious. He discovered the self archetype after all his intensive studies and writings on the other archetypes were completed. He concluded that "... the self is our life's goal, for it is the completest expression of that fateful combination we call individuality ..." (Vol. 7, p. 238).

V. INTERACTIONS AMONG THE STRUCTURES OF PERSONALITY

The discussion of Jung's structural concepts, one by one, suggests that they are separate and distinct from each other. Such is not the case, however; there are many interactions among them. Jung discusses three kinds of interactions. One structure may *compensate* for the weakness of another structure, one component may *oppose* another component, and two or more structures may *unite* to form a synthesis.

Compensation may be illustrated by the contrasting attitudes of extraversion and introversion. If extraversion is the dominant or superior attitude of the conscious ego, then the unconscious will compensate by developing the repressed attitude of introversion. This means that if the extraverted attitude is frustrated in some way, the unconscious inferior attitude of introversion will come to the fore and exert itself in behavior. That is why a period of intense extraverted behavior is ordinarily followed by a period of introverted behavior. The unconscious always compensates for weaknesses in the personality system.

Compensation also occurs between functions. A person who stresses thinking or feeling in his conscious mind will be an intuitive, sensation type unconsciously. Likewise, the ego and the anima in a man and the ego and the animus in a woman bear a compensatory relationship to each other. The normal male ego is masculine while the anima is feminine, and the normal female ego is feminine while the animus is masculine. The principle of compensation provides for a kind of equilibrium or balance between contrasting elements which prevents the psyche from becoming neurotically unbalanced.

Virtually all personality theorists of whatever creed or persuasion assume that the personality contains polar tendencies that may come into conflict with one another. Jung is no exception. He believes that a psychological theory of personality must be founded on the principle of opposition or conflict because the tensions created by conflicting elements are the very essence of life itself. Without tension there would be no energy and consequently no personality.

Opposition exists everywhere in the personality: between the persona and the shadow, between the persona and the anima, and between the shadow and the anima. Introversion opposes extraversion, thinking opposes feeling, and sensation opposes intuition. The ego is like a shuttlecock that is batted back and forth between the outer demands of society and the inner demands of the collective unconscious. The woman in man contends with the man in man, and the animus contends with the femininity of woman. The contest between the rational and irrational forces of the psyche never ceases. Conflict is a ubiquitous fact of life. The important issue is whether these conflicts will lead to the shattering of a personality or whether they can be tolerated and endured. In the former case, the person becomes a victim of neurosis or psychosis. He becomes mad or nearly mad. If conflicts can be tolerated, they may provide the motive power for creative achievement, and lend a liveliness to the person's behavior.

Must personality always be a house divided against itself? Jung thought not. There can always be a union of opposites, a theme that looms very large in Jung's writings. Again and again, he offers evidence of the various ways in which opposites can be synthesized. The union of opposites is accomplished by what Jung called the *transcendent function.* (See Chapter Four.) It is this inborn function that leads to the formation of a balanced, integrated personality.

VI. SUMMARY

We have now come to the end of our discussion of Jung's structural concepts. It will be recognized that as seen through Jung's eyes the personality is an exceedingly complex structure. Not only are there numerous components—the number of possible archetypes and complexes is legion—but also the interactions among these components are intricate and involved. But then no thoughtful person has ever regarded the personality as being a simple structure. Jung's structural concepts try to confer order on what appears to be a conglomeration of human mental states and actions.

When one tries to comprehend the ways in which the components of personality express themselves in an individual human being the task becomes extremely difficult. The reason for this is that one has to assess the strength of the components at any given moment of time *and* also the variations in strength that occur over time. The psyche is not a stable fixed thing like a rock or even a tree that can be described once and for all. It is a dynamic system which is constantly changing. In the next chapter we will describe Jung's dynamic concepts.

REFERENCES

Jung, C. G. *Collected Works.* Princeton, N. J.: Princeton University Press.
Vol. 7. *Two Essays on Analytical Psychology.*

Vol. 8. *The Structure and Dynamics of the Psyche.*
Vol. 9i. *The Archetypes and the Collective Unconscious.*
Vol. 10. *Civilization in Transition.*
Vol. 15. *The Spirit in Man, Art, and Literature*
Vol. 17. *The Development of Personality.*
JUNG, C. G. *Memories, Dreams, Reflections.* New York: Vintage Books, 1961.

CHAPTER THREE

The Dynamics of Personality

In order for the personality structures described in the preceding chapter to carry on their activities, they must be energized. Where does this energy come from? What is its nature? How is it utilized? How does it distribute itself among the various structures of personality? These are the questions we will be concerned with in the present chapter.

I. THE PSYCHE: A RELATIVELY CLOSED SYSTEM

To begin with, Jung proposes that the total personality or psyche is a *relatively closed system*. By describing it as being relatively closed he means that it must be dealt with as a unitary system within itself; that is, a more or less self-contained energy system, apart from any other energy system. Although the psyche receives energy or is energized by external sources, including the body, this energy once it is added belongs exclusively to the psyche. In other words, the fate of this added energy is determined by an already existing energy system which is the psyche, and not by the nature of the external sources. The psyche might be described as a sphere of an impermeable nature except for its inlets through which new energy is added to the system from external sources.

The energy contributed from external sources is derived from the things we touch, see, smell, taste, feel, or hear. These senses provide a continuous source of stimulation by which the psyche is fed, much as the food we eat feeds the body. This is the reason why the psychic system is in a continuously changing state and why it can never attain a state of perfect equilibrium. It can only achieve relative stability. Stimuli from the external environment and from the body produce a never-ending redistribution or shifting of energy within the system. *If* the psyche were a totally closed system, it *could* reach a state of perfect balance, for it would not be subjected to interference from the outside. In this case, the psyche would be like a pool of water, soon to become stagnant from the lack of fresh water.

It is not necessary to belabor this point. The reader has certainly experienced many times the situation where everything seems to be running along smoothly when some unexpected and unforeseen event throws him off balance. The slightest stimulus may have far-reaching consequences on one's mental stability. This shows that it is not the amount of energy that is added, but the disruptive effects that the added energy produces within the psyche. These disruptive effects are caused by massive redistributions of energy within the system. It takes only the slightest pressure on the trigger of a loaded gun to cause a great disaster. Similarly, it may take only the slightest addition of energy to an unstable psyche to produce large effects in a person's behavior. An innocuous remark can, for example, produce an overheated emotional reaction in the person to whom it is addressed.

It is folly, Jung would say, to think that a person can prepare himself for every possible contingency. New experiences will crowd into the psyche and disrupt its balance. That is why Jung prescribes a periodic withdrawal from the world in order to recover one's balance. Meditation is one such method of withdrawing into oneself and shutting out the world. A more drastic method, and one that is not recommended, is complete and permanent withdrawal, which is technically known as autism or catatonia. The catatonic person is impervious to virtually all forms of stimulation.

On the other hand, there is also a need for stimulation or novelty. A person's life may become so routine and cut off from new experiences that he succumbs to boredom and inertia. In such cases, a jolt from the external world will activate the psyche and induce a feeling of vigor and vivacity.

If the psyche were completely open, there would be chaos; if the psyche were completely closed, it would stagnate. The healthy, well-stabilized personality functions within a middle area between these two extremes.

II. PSYCHIC ENERGY

The energy by which the work of the personality is performed is called *psychic energy*. Jung also used the word *libido* for this form of energy, but it is not to be confused with Freud's definition of libido. Jung did not restrict libido to sexual energy as Freud did. In fact, this is one of the essential differences in the theories of the two men. Libido in its natural state is appetite, according to Jung—the appetites of hunger, thirst, and sex, as well as the emotions. Libido is manifested consciously as striving, desiring, and willing.

Psychic energy cannot be measured quantitatively in terms of formulae as forms of physical energy can be. For example, radiation can be measured in rads or electricity in volts. Psychic energy expresses itself in the form either of actual or of potential forces which perform psychological work. Perceiving, remembering, thinking, feeling, wishing, willing, attending, and striving are psychological activities just as breathing, digesting, and perspiring are physiological activities. Potential forces of the personality are such things as predispositions, latent tendencies, and inclinations. These potential or latent forces may be activated at any time.

Psychic energy, as we have said, originates from the experiences that a person has. Just as food is consumed by the physical body and is converted into biological or life energy, so experiences are "consumed" by the psyche and are converted into psychic energy.

Except in rare instances of physical shocks to the brain, the psyche, just like the body, is always doing something. Even when we are deeply asleep the psyche is still actively producing dreams. We may not always be aware of these activities, any more than we are aware of all of our physiological activities, but this does not mean they are not taking place. We remember only a few of our dreams, yet recent evidence suggests that we dream continuously throughout the night. It is very difficult for people to accept this view of a continuously active psyche, because there is a strong tendency to equate psychic activity with conscious activity. Jung, as well as Freud, hammered away at this misconception, but it persists even today.

Jung points out that it is impossible to prove scientifically that there is a relationship of equivalence between physical and psychical energy. He believes, however, that there is some sort of reciprocal action between the two systems. That is to say, psychic energy is converted into physical energy, and physical energy is converted into psychic energy. It is certainly true, for example, that drugs which produce chemical effects in the body also produce changes in psychological functioning. And thoughts and feelings appear to affect physiological functions. This is the whole basis on which psychosomatic medicine is founded. Jung may be regarded as one of the forerunners of this important new conception in medicine.

III. PSYCHIC VALUES

One of Jung's most important dynamic concepts is that of *value*. A value is a measure of the amount of energy that is committed to a particular psychic element. When a high value is placed upon an idea or feeling it means that this idea or feeling exerts considerable force in influencing and directing one's behavior. A person who places a high value on beauty will devote large amounts of energy to seeking beauty, surrounding himself with beautiful objects, traveling to places where beauty may be found, associating with beautiful people and animals, and, if he has the capabilities, producing beautiful works of art. A person who does not value beauty will do none of these things. He will use little or no energy for esthetic enjoyment. He may, on the other hand, place a high value on power and consign lots of energy to activities that gain him power.

The absolute value of psychic energy that is invested in a psychological element cannot be determined, but its value relative to other values can be. We can weigh or compare our psychic values against one another and determine their relative strengths. We may ask ourselves whether we prefer truth or beauty, power or knowledge, wealth or friends, and so forth. Or better yet we can observe ourselves or others and see how much time and energy are devoted to various activities. If one spends forty hours a week earning money and one hour a week enjoying the beauties of nature, it is not difficult to judge the relative values of these two activities. Another way to proceed in establishing relative values is to offer a person a choice of different things, and note which he chooses. Still another method is to place obstacles in his path to a goal and observe how long he persists in trying to overcome the obstacles. A person with a weak value for the goal in question quickly gives up. A person may quite accurately discover his values by keeping a record of his dreams. If he has many sex dreams and few dreams of seeking power, we can be fairly confident that sex ranks higher in his scale of values than power does.

The psyche as a dynamic system is constantly evaluating. That is, various amounts of energy are assigned to various psychological activities. The amounts assigned vary from time to time. Today we may dedicate a lot of energy to studying for an examination, tomorrow we may devote a lot of energy to playing tennis or riding horseback. One's scale of values does not remain in a constant pattern.

The observations and methods for estimating the relative strength of values are indicative of conscious values, but they do not provide much information about the unconscious values. If a conscious value disappears without appearing in any other equivalent conscious activity, one can expect this value to appear in the unconscious, on the assumption that energy is not lost from the system. Since the regions of the unconscious are not directly accessible for observation, auxiliary methods must be employed for assessing unconscious values. One such method consists of determining the constellating power of a complex.

A complex, as described in the last chapter, consists of a central or nuclear element around which a large number of secondary associations are grouped. The number of such associations is a measure of the constellating or attracting power of the complex. The greater the constellating power the greater the value or strength of the complex. For example, if one has a "strong leader"

61

complex it means that the nucleus, the need to rule others, will draw to it many experiences or associations. The total constellation may consist of such things as admiration of heroes, identification with outstanding people, assuming responsibilities others evade, getting decisions accepted and approved by people, being consulted on matters both trivial and paramount, expression of one's ideas on every possible occasion, and seeking respect and admiration. Each new experience will tend to get itself assimilated into the leader complex. Jung writes, "One complex has a higher value when its power of assimilation proves stronger than that of another."

What methods are used for assessing the energic value of the constellating power of a complex? Jung proposed three methods. These are (1) direct observations plus analytical deductions, (2) complex indicators, and (3) the intensity of emotional expression.

A DIRECT OBSERVATION AND DEDUCTION

A complex does not always exhibit its characteristics in conscious behavior. It may appear in the form of dreams, or in disguised forms so it is necessary to pay attention to circumstantial evidence in order to uncover its significance. That is what is meant by analytical deduction. For example, a person may appear to be very subservient and submissive in his relations with others. But then it is noticed that such a person seems always to get his way. He is the sort of person who says "Don't bother about me" and immediately everyone does bother about him. Or "You go right ahead; I'll stay home if there isn't room," and everyone rushes around to see that the person does go even if someone else has to be left out. Or the mother who sacrifices herself to her family and then becomes an invalid so that she has to be waited on and pampered. Control over others (the power complex) is exercised by manipulating them in subtle ways, for which the person cannot be criticized because he or she is *so* self-effacing and self-sacrificing.

Any strongly negative attitude toward something may hide a positive interest in the very thing one is vociferously rejecting. The person who says, "I can't stand gossips" may be the one who gossips most. Or one who says "I don't care about the pay, I just like the work" may be the first one to complain about insufficient pay. Analytical psychologists learn not to take all statements at their face value, but to see what lies behind them.

B. COMPLEX INDICATORS   Any disturbance of behavior may be indicative of a complex. For example, a person may call someone he knows very well by the wrong name. When a man calls his wife by his mother's name, it suggests that his mother complex has assimilated his wife to it. Or it can be a blockage of memory for something that we know very well. The repressed memory, it is assumed, has some connection with an unconscious complex so that the memory is swallowed up by it. An exaggerated emotional reaction to a situation indicates that the situation is connected in some way to a complex.

As previously mentioned, Jung's use of the word-association test was an attempt to elicit complex indicators under laboratory conditions. He was able to estimate the value intensity of a complex by the delay in response to a word and by other peculiarities of the reaction to a test word.

Jung states that a complex is more difficult to uncover when there is overcompensation. Overcompensation is when the nucleus of a complex is obscured by another complex which temporarily has a higher energic value. It has this higher value because the person has deliberately shifted energy from the "real" complex to a "disguising" complex. An example of this is a man who has an inferiority complex about his masculine virility, and who overcompensates by developing and exhibiting his physique, boasting of his virility and sexual prowess, and rejecting anything that seems to him to be feminine. He is the sort of person who censures effeminate men because they remind him of his own felt inferiority.

Another example is the person who commits a crime because he has a guilt complex. He hopes to be apprehended and even carefully arranges it so that he will be apprehended, in order to be arrested and punished. The punishment serves to relieve his guilt complex, at least temporarily. One can see this occur in children who willfully misbehave. They are often motivated by a need for punishment rather than by aggression.

Once the real complex has been identified, it can be dealt with. As long as one tries to treat the "disguising" complex, little progress can be made.

C. EMOTIONAL REACTIONS   We have already mentioned that exaggerated emotional reactions point to an underlying complex. Jung also studied the expression of emotion under laboratory conditions. He used measures of changes in the pulse rate, fluctuations in breathing, and changes in the electrical conductivity of the skin produced by emotional sweating, in conjunction with the word-association test. If any of these changes occurred when a word was given, it indicated that a complex had been tapped. Other words belonging to the same general category could then be introduced to see whether they evoked emotional responses also.

D. INTUITION   In addition to the aforementioned tests, experiments, analyses, and observations, Jung believed there was another way of recognizing a complex. That is the natural and spontaneous capacity every man has to perceive the slightest emotional fluctuation in others. This capacity is called intuition. It is more highly developed in some people than in others. Intuition becomes more sensitive and more accurate as our familiarity with a person increases. Two people who have an intense relationship can recognize almost immediately when one or the other is under the domination of a complex.

IV. THE PRINCIPLE OF EQUIVALENCE

Psychodynamics is concerned with the distribution of energy throughout the structures of the psyche, and the transfer of energy from one structure to another. Jungian psychodynamics makes use of two basic principles, both of which were derived from physics. They are the *principle of equivalence* and the *principle of entropy*.

The principle of equivalence states that if the amount of energy consigned to a given psychic element decreases or disappears, that amount of energy will appear in another psychic element. That is, no energy is lost from the psyche; it is simply transferred from one position to another. Actually, the energy may be distributed amongst several components. Students of physics will recognize that this principle of equivalence is the first law of thermodynamics or the conservation of energy.

An analogy may help to make the operation of this principle clearer. If a person pays ten dollars for a pair of shoes, that amount of money obviously does not disappear. It is distributed eventually among a number of people: the owner of the store, the clerks, and other personnel, the wholesaler and his employees, the manufacturer and his employees, the producer of the leather, a variety of tax collectors, etc. etc. In exactly the same manner, the energy in one value is transferred to another value or a lot of different values. The transference itself does not use up any energy any more than handing a clerk ten dollars decreases the value of the ten dollars.

One does not need to resort to analogies, however, because it is readily apparent that the psyche does not stop doing something without doing something else in its place. We expect, for example, that when a boy begins to lose interest in model airplanes, comic books, and playing cops and robbers he will begin to take an interest in automobiles, novels, and girls. Loss of interest in something always means a gain of interest in something else. Even when we are tired and fall asleep, the mind keeps on churning out very complex hallucinations. The energy that we use for thinking, feeling, and acting during the day is transferred to dreaming during the night.

Sometimes, however, sums of psychic energy seem to disappear instead of being transferred. In such cases, energy has been transferred from the conscious ego to the personal unconscious or to the collective unconscious. The structures that make up both of these levels of the unconscious require energy, and often a great deal of energy, in order to conduct their activities. As we have said, these activities cannot be directly observed; they must be inferred from the actions of the person. A well-known example of this transformation from consciousness to the unconscious takes place when a child starts to become independent of his parents. He then begins to have fantasies of substitute parents which are sooner or later projected on real people, such as a teacher, a coach, or an older friend of his parents. This illustrates how the unconscious value has the same characteristics the conscious value had. The child's valuation of his parents disappeared when he separated himself from them; this value then became unconscious and manifested itself in the form of fantasies; then it became conscious once again with new objects but still retaining a value very similar to the original value. We can be quite sure that if a person suddenly changes his character (from a Dr. Jekyll to a Mr. Hyde), a redistribution of values is responsible for the transformation. Less dramatic and therefore less obvious influences of unconscious values on behavior are continually taking place. Many of these unconscious values are responsible for the contents of our dreams. Unconscious values are also responsible for the appearance of neurotic symptoms such as phobias, obsessions, and compulsions, and psychotic symptoms such as hallucinations, delusions, and extreme withdrawal from reality. That is why the psychodynamics of personality are often seen to best advantage in a mental hospital or a psychiatrist's office. But as Jung pointed out repeatedly, they can also be seen in a wide variety of social phenomena, such as crime, war, prejudice, and discrimination, and in art, mythology, religion, and occultism.

Given a personality system that has a finite amount of energy available to it at any one time, it follows that there will be competition among the various structures for this energy. If one structure obtains more, there will be that much less available for the other structures. Again an analogy from everyday experience will illustrate this. A person has so much money to spend each month. He cannot buy everything he wants, so he has to decide how he will apportion the money among his various needs and desires. In the same manner, the psychic system has to "decide" how it will apportion energy among the various structures. Actually, these "decisions" are made by another dynamic principle which we will discuss in a moment.

Jung also points out that in transferring energy from one structure to another, some characteristics of the first structure are transferred to the second structure. For example, if energy from a power complex passes into a sexual complex, some aspects of the value placed on power will appear in the sexual values. When this happens, a person's sexual behavior will contain some features of a need to dominate his sexual partners. Jung warns us, however, not to make the assumption that all of the characteristics of the first complex are transferred. The second complex still exhibits its own character. Jung says, "It may be that the libido of some spiritual activity goes over into an essentially material interest, whereupon the individual erroneously believes that the new structure is equally spiritual in character" (Vol. 8, p. 21). There may be similarities, Jung notes, but there are also essential differences.

As a general rule, psychic energy can be transferred from one structure to another only on the basis of equivalence. That is, if a person has an intense attachment to a person, object, or activity, it can only be replaced by something of an equally intense value. Sometimes, however, not all of the energy will be used by the new value; in that case, the excess energy will go into an unconscious element.

Up to this point our discussion of equivalence has pertained primarily to single elements or psychic values. Now we would like to discuss how the principle of equivalence functions with respect to the major structures of personality—the ego, anima, shadow, etc. The principle remains the same, although the effects on behavior may be much more significant than is the case with single values. If a large quantity of psychic energy should be removed from the ego and added to the persona, the effects would be very evident in a person's behavior. He would no longer be "himself" but instead he would be the person that he thinks others want him to be. His personality would take on an increasingly masklike character.

Once a system becomes highly developed, it will seize all possible energy from the other systems. This is difficult to do when the energy is bound to another system, but quite easily accomplished when there is loose energy or when energy is in the process of flowing from one system to another.

Although in the above example we illustrated how psychic energy could flow from the ego to the persona, the energy does not always redistribute itself in such a direct manner as this. It is possible for the ego to become de-energized, and for that energy to redistribute itself into *several* of the other personality systems, instead of into just one system. Nor should one forget that because new energy is constantly being added to the psyche from outside sources, it can be responsible for increasing the energy levels in any of the systems. It is this continual process of energy input as well as the distribution and redistribution of energy *within* the psyche that intrigued Jung so. As a result of this interest Jung's analytical psychology is a truly dynamic psychology.

In summary, then, the principle of equivalence states that whenever psychic energy is transferred from one element or structure of the psyche to another element or structure, the value of the energy will remain the same. Psychic energy cannot disappear; it can be added to the psyche by experiences but it cannot be subtracted from the psyche.

V. THE PRINCIPLE OF ENTROPY

The equivalence principle describes the exchanges of energy within a system, but it does not account for the *direction* in which the energy will flow. Why does energy flow, let us say, from the ego into the persona rather than into the shadow or anima? It is like asking a person why he bought a pair of shoes rather than a book or a box of candy. The person would probably reply, "Because I need shoes more than I need a book or candy." This answer also applies to energy exchanges within the psyche. Energy flows from the ego to the persona because the persona "needs" it more than the anima or the shadow does. It "needs" it because it has less energy than the ego or the anima or the shadow.

The direction in which energy flows is conceptualized in physics by the second law of thermodynamics, which is called the principle of entropy. This principle states, in effect, that when two bodies of different temperatures are placed in contact, heat (thermal energy) will pass from the hotter to the colder body until the temperature of the two bodies is equalized. Another example is that of the flow of water between two containers, which is always in the direction of moving from a higher level to a lower level, when a channel is available, until the water level is the same in the two containers. Generalizing, energy will always flow from a stronger body to a weaker body when they are accessible to each other. The operation of the entropy principle results in an equilibrium of forces.

The principle of entropy as adapted by Jung to describe personality dynamics states that the distribution of energy in the psyche seeks an equilibrium or balance among all the structures of the psyche. To take the simplest case, if two values (energy intensities) are of unequal strength, energy will tend to pass from the stronger value into the weaker value until a balance is reached. On a larger scale, entropy governs the exchanges of energy throughout the whole personality, with the aim of achieving a completely balanced system. Naturally, this aim is never fully realized, and it may be pointed out that if it were, there would be no more exchanges of energy and the psyche would cease to function. It would be frozen just as the physical world would be frozen if perfect entropy ever took place. Everything would stop.

It cannot happen to the psyche because the psyche is not a completely closed system. This means that new energy is always being added to the psyche from external sources. This added energy creates imbalances. When the personality dynamics are relatively quiescent because there is some degree of equilibrium among the structures, any new stimulation may upset the balance, and the feelings of quiescence are replaced by feelings of tension and conflict. Tension, conflict, stress, and strain are all feelings that arise from imbalances in the psyche. The greater the inequities in energy among the structures, the greater is the tension and the conflict that the person experiences. A person may feel that he is being torn to pieces by these inner conflicts, and sometimes that happens. Personalities can become shattered when the tensions are extremely great, just as a volcano can erupt when the pressure (tension) is extremely great.

However, as Jung points out, the equalization of two values or structures that originally had very unequal amounts of energy—one very low, the other very high— can lead to a strong durable synthesis of the values or structures which will be difficult to sunder. Imagine, for example, a man with a strong shadow and a weak anima. The weak anima tries to draw energy from the powerful shadow. But as energy is taken from the shadow more energy is added to it from external sources. So the conflict rages, one-sided though it may be. If the conflict is ultimately resolved so that some sort of balance between the two structures is achieved, this balance will, according to Jung, be difficult to disturb. The union of opposites (shadow versus anima), under such circumstances, will be a particularly strong one. Instead of being compulsively masculine, the man will express in his behavior a blend, let us say, of virility and tenderness, of strength and compassion, of determination and sentiment. Such an outcome is fortunate, but too often the conflict continues and the opposites are not united.

The strong bond that can be established between opposing structures like the shadow and the anima has its counterpart in human relationships. The strongest relationship often develops between two persons who originally were strongly opposed to one another. They have had to fight through a lot of battles but there comes a day when all of the battles have been settled and an enduring friendship is firmly cemented. This, too, is not a typical outcome. Either the fighting continues or it gets worse and the relationship is terminated.

The comparison between intrapsychic conflicts and interpersonal conflicts is not just an analogy, however, because, as Jung points out, our conflicts with other people (or for that matter with animals and objects) are often, if not always, projections of conflicts within our own personality. A husband who fights with his wife is fighting with his own anima. A person who campaigns vigorously, even fanatically, against what he regards as sin and immorality is fighting his own shadow.

As we have said, stimulation from external sources may produce tension and strain in the psyche by adding energy to it. Under normal conditions, this new energy can be accommodated within the psyche without causing serious dislocations. But if the psyche is already unstable, due to an uneven distribution of energy, and if the stimulation is so strong that it cannot be handled, the person may protect himself by building a shell around himself. In his mental-hospital experience, Jung observed a dulling of the emotions in psychotic patients. They did not respond with feeling to situations that ordinarily call forth an emotional response. It is only when this shell is penetrated that feeling erupts, often violently.

More normal people have ways of protecting themselves from disturbing situations. They close their minds, as one says, and refuse to listen to anything that will disturb their convictions. They often have deeply ingrained prejudices. They are conservative and resist change because they feel secure and comfortable with a settled state of mind. By closing their minds to new experiences, they can come closer to a state of perfect entropy, which, as we have said, can only occur in a closed system.

We often speak of the "storms of youth" and the "tranquillity of age." The turbulence of youth is due to the vast amount of energy that pours into the psyche both from external and bodily sources. Consider, for example, the physiological changes that take place at puberty, as well as the many new experiences that the young person encounters as the ties with his family begin to weaken. The principle of entropy cannot function fast enough to deal adequately with the great amount of energy being brought into the psyche. The psychic values cannot reach a state of equilibrium simply because new values are continually being created by new experiences. The principle of entropy will immediately proceed to deal with the new value that has been created, but before the process is complete, other values will appear as a result of new experiences. Or perhaps two values have reached some sort of balance when a third value appears which causes a redistribution of energy between the first two values. Feelings of uncertainty, bewilderment, conflict, insecurity, anxiety, and confusion get projected out in the form of rebellion, moodiness, unpredictability, and impulsiveness. What else could one expect, Jung might say, from the chaotic ebb and flow of energies within the youthful psyche.

With regard to the so-called "tranquillity of age," age really has no bearing on it. It is the experiences that one has had and which have been dealt with and incorporated into the personality with some degree of harmony which results in tranquillity. A new experience is not as upsetting for an older person because it adds less new energy relative to the total amount of energy in the psyche than it does for a younger person.

There is another obstacle to the operation of the entropy principle in the personality dynamics. When a structure becomes highly developed and consequently assumes a position of great power in the psyche, it tends to become independent of and cut off from the rest of the psyche. Like an autocratic ruler, it seizes more and more power (energy) from other structures, besides monopolizing new energy that enters the psyche. The flow of energy from a strong structure to a weak one is not only blocked; it is reversed. Thus, the psyche becomes greatly unbalanced; there is one dominant structure which becomes stronger and a lot of weak ones which become weaker. A strong complex, for example, will attract a great many of the new experiences to it, just as a rich and powerful nation tends to become richer and more powerful by appropriating or discovering new sources of wealth. This sort of autocracy in the personality may be a stabilizing influence, for a time, but there is always the danger that the ruling complex will be overthrown by the operation of the entropy principle. The sudden flow of energy out of a powerful system can have the same disastrous consequences that result from the breaking of a dam.

Jung points out that every extreme state secretly contains its opposite, and that the sudden conversion of a very dominant value into its opposite often occurs. This means, for example, that a person with a strong power complex can suddenly become very subservient and submissive. Or a person with a highly developed persona drops his mask and becomes a menace to society. As a psychoanalyst, Jung had many opportunities to observe abrupt transformations in the personalities of his patients. These spectacular changes in personality and behavior are due to the operation of the entropy principle. The energy that has accumulated in such large quantities in a complex or other structure suddenly drains out of the complex and is deposited in its opposite. For this reason, overdeveloped structures are invariably unstable.

The psychological counterpart of the principle of entropy is the *self*. The self, it will be recalled, is an archetype whose function is to integrate the various structures of the personality. And as we shall see in the next chapter, Jung proposes still a third integrating function, the *transcendent function*.

VI. PROGRESSION AND REGRESSION

One of the most important concepts of psychodynamics is the progression and regression of psychic energy. Progression is defined as a person's daily experiences which advance his psychological adaptation. Although some personalities appear as though their psychological advancement is completely achieved, this is mistaking a person's conscious behavior for his actual psychic adaptation. One's progression is a continuous proc ss since his environment and experiences change continuously; therefore, his adaptation is never completely achieved.

The progression of libido can be said to be in accordance with the demands of environmental conditions. From the very beginning of life, one meets the world with a predisposition to exercise a particular mental function. By beginning with a particular orientation, the psyche has a one-sidedness in its direction. If the one-sidedness of this function becomes *too* dominant, *too* powerful, through the process of progression it will draw every possible experience and psychic energy to itself. But there will come a time when this function no longer is adaptive, and a new function is called for. For example, if feeling is the dominant function, new situations may require a thinking orientation for proper adaptation, thus making feeling inappropriate for these situations. In this case the feeling attitude would lose its strength and the progression of psychic energy in that function would cease. The certainty and assuredness that were present before dissolve, and is replaced by an assortment of chaotic psychic values. The person is "all at sea." Subjective contents and reactions accumulate, and the psyche becomes full of tension.

In order for progression of libido to be reinstated, it is necessary that the pair of opposite functions, in this case feeling and thinking, be united. Thinking and feeling must reach a state of interaction and mutual influence, thus preventing the psychic functions from becoming unbalanced in their development. If this is not done, psychic energy comes to a standstill and the pair of opposites cannot be coordinated.

The struggle between the opposites would continue indefinitely if the process of *regression* did not step in to interrupt the conflict. Regression is the backward movement of libido. Through the collision and interactions of the opposites, they steadily become deprived of their energy (they are said to be depotentiated) by the process of regression. Regression *subtracts* energy from psychic elements whereas progression *adds* energy to psychic elements. During this crisis, through the process of regression, there is a steady loss of value of the opposites, and gradually the new function can evolve. This newly developed function asserts itself at first only indirectly on our conscious behavior. Continuing our example, then, this new function is thinking which is replacing feeling.

Thinking then is the new function activated by regression, and upon reaching consciousness it appears somewhat foreign, disguised, and crude in form, or as Jung picturesquely describes it, it "will be covered with the slime of the deep" (Vol. 8, p. 34). The "deep" refers to the deep unconscious state from which the thinking function was summoned. While feeling was the predominant function everything was oriented to that function; elements were carefully excluded from interacting with any other function such as the thinking function. Thus the thinking function never had an opportunity to develop; it remained unused, untrained, and undifferentiated as long as the feeling function was predominant.

By activating an unconscious function by regression, the new function is faced with problems of outward adaptation. Once the new function achieves its initial adaptation, progression of libido can commence once again. Through progression the new thinking orientation can develop a sense of certainty and assuredness, just as the previous feeling orientation developed a sense of assuredness by daily progression.

Adaptation is not only necessitated by events in the outer world; a person must also adapt to his inner psychic world. To continue our example, if feeling is the dominant function then the person's orientation to his own unconscious will be in the thinking mode. This may suffice, at first, but in the long run it will not always be adequate and the feeling function will have to be enlisted too, just as the reverse was necessary when dealing with the external world.

Jung states that man "can meet the demands of outer necessity in an ideal way only if he is adapted to his own inner world, that is, if he is in harmony with himself. Conversely, he can only adapt to his inner world and achieve harmony with himself when he is adapted to the environmental conditions" (Vol. 8, p. 39). The interdependence of these two kinds of adaptation means that a person cannot neglect one without injuring the other. Regrettably, outer adjustment is stressed in modern life without realizing that it cannot be achieved in the absence of inner adjustment. Progression and regression are both essential for good adjustment.

Jung also points out that regression can be beneficial because it activates the archetypes which contain a great deal of racial wisdom. This racial wisdom will often enable the person to solve the immediate problems facing him in his present life. For example, the hero archetype can provide a person with the courage he needs to deal with a critical and incapacitating situation. Periods of withdrawal or retreats are recommended by Jung, not in order to escape from life's problems, but in order to renew one's energies from the reservoir in the unconscious. We do this every night when we sleep. Sleep provides an opportunity for a descent into the unconscious and for the manifestations of the unconscious in dreams. Unfortunately, modern man does not pay sufficient attention to the power and wisdom inherent in his dreams.

Jung cautions us not to confuse *progression* with *development*. The former refers to the direction in which energy flows; the latter to differentiation (individuation) of structures. Regression and progression are analogous to the ebb and flow of the tide. Of course, progression or regression by activating structures can indirectly influence development.

Nor should progression and regression be confused with extraversion and introversion, which superficially they seem to resemble. Actually, progression and regression may each occur in either an extraverted or introverted form. Progression and regression are energy concepts and not formal structures or elements of the psyche, which were described in the last chapter.

VII. CANALIZATION OF ENERGY

Psychical energy, like physical energy, becomes channeled, converted, and transformed, or to use Jung's term, it becomes *canalized*.

It may help to clarify the concept of canalization by describing some parallels with physical energy. A waterfall may be a beautiful thing to look at, but aside from its esthetic value, it is of little use to man in its natural form. When some of the water from the top of the waterfall is diverted into downflowing pipes to the turbines in a power plant, electricity is generated. This electricity is conducted over lines to be used for a multitude of purposes. Man has always harnessed energy to perform work for him. Some of his techniques are fairly simple, like using the wind to propel a sailboat, wood and coal to produce heat, and water to turn a waterwheel. Others are more complex, like the use of gasoline or other fuel to operate the combustion engine and steam turbine, and more recently nuclear power plants. The body converts the energy from food into muscle energy. The psyche also converts or canalizes energy. Let us see how this is done, according to Jung.

The source of natural energy is the instincts. This instinctual energy follows its own course or gradient like the waterfall does, but it does not perform any work, no more than a waterfall does. This natural energy must be diverted into new channels in order for work to be done. "Just as a power station imitates a waterfall and thereby gains possession of its energy, so the psychic mechanism imitates the instinct and is thereby enabled to apply its energy for special purposes ... The transformation of instinctual energy is achieved by its canalization into an *analogue of the object of instinct*" (Vol. 8, p. 42; Jung's emphasis). This analogue is what Jung means by a *symbol*. The power station is a symbol of the waterfall.

Let us pause to see what Jung means by work. A person who lives a perfectly instinctual life—that is, natural man as contrasted with civilized man—would live each moment in accordance with the demands of his instincts just as animals do. He would eat when hungry, drink when thirsty, copulate when sexually aroused, run when frightened, strike when angered, and sleep when tired. He would follow the gradient of his instinctual energy just as a river follows a descending gradient through the countryside, or smoke follows an ascending gradient, or salmon swim upstream to spawn, or some birds migrate south in the winter.

In a natural state man would have no culture, no symbolic forms, no technical developments, no social organizations, no schools or churches, etc. When natural energy is diverted into cultural or symbolic channels this is what Jung means by work.

How does this diversion take place? By imitation or analogy-making, Jung says. Something is like something else. For example, the origin of the physical concept of force is to be found in the perception of our own muscular power.

An example of canalization is the spring ceremony performed by an Australian tribe. "They dig a hole in the ground, oval in shape and set about with bushes so that it looks like a woman's genitals. Then they dance round this hole, holding their spears in front of them in imitation of an erect penis. As they dance round, they thrust their spears into the hole, shouting (English equivalent) 'Not a pit, not a pit, but a cunt' ... There can be no doubt that this is a canalization of energy and its transference to an analogue of the original object by means of the dance and by imitating the sexual act" (Vol. 8, pp. 42-43).

Many other examples of canalization might be cited. The buffalo dance of the Pueblo Indians prepares young men for the hunt. The Aruntas tribe of Australia performs a ceremony when one of their members has been murdered by another tribe. The hair of the deceased is tied to the mouth and penis of those men who have been chosen to avenge the murder. This angers them, thus providing an additional incentive to find the murderer. There are many similar ceremonies among primitive people: ceremonies and dances to ensure the fertility of the soil, to bring rain, for protection from evil spirits, to prepare for war, to increase a woman's fertility, and to gain strength, power, and good health. The complexity of these ceremonies shows how much attention is required to divert psychic energy from its natural flow of everyday habit into some new activity. It is comparable to the effort that is needed to convert water power into electrical power.

The value of these ceremonies is that they direct attention to the task to be undertaken—the killing of buffaloes or the planting of crops—and thereby increase the chances of success. The ceremonies act as a sort of programming process to prepare a person psychologically for the task he is about to perform.

It is important to bear in mind, Jung tells us, that the symbol, although it is *like* the original, is not *identical* with it. The flow of a river within its banks is like the flow of electricity along a wire, but electricity is not the same as flowing water. Dancing resembles sexual intercourse, but it is not sexual intercourse. The boring of wood to make fire is analogous to the sex act, but it is not the sex act. Cultural and technical activities have their origins in analogies with instinctual activities, but once they are developed or invented they have their own independent qualities and characteristics. We shall have a great deal more to say about man's propensity for symbol-making in Chapter Six.

Jung observes that modern man depends more upon *will* than upon ceremony. He decides to do something and does it or learns how to do it. He does not waste his time in dancing or chanting, except as recreations, although Jung quickly points out that modern man resorts to rituals and magic when he feels insecure about the success of some new venture.

These "acts of will" also produce analogues (symbols) of the original instincts. These analogous objects or activities have a stimulating or inspirational effect on the imagination, so the psyche is preoccupied, fascinated, and possessed by them. This provides the incentive for the mind to perform all kinds of operations on the object, and to make discoveries about it that it would not have noticed otherwise. Jung notes that modern science is an outgrowth of primitive magic. The age of science enabled the magical dreams of controlling natural phenomena to come true. By channeling energy from the instincts into scientific symbols of the instincts, man has been able to make over the world. As Jung says, "... we have every reason ... to render homage to the symbol as an inestimable means of utilizing the mere instinctual flow of energy for effective work" (Vol. 8, p. 47).

In physical nature only a very small amount of natural

energy can be transformed into effective working energy, which leaves the far greater portion in its natural state. The same condition applies to instinctual energy; only a small portion can be diverted to symbol-making. The greater part continues its natural flow to sustain the regular course of life. The only time we can successfully transform a portion of the libido (psychic energy) by an "act of will" is when we devise a strong symbol that will divert the energy to it.

Although the libido is used exclusively for sustaining the personality system, a certain amount of energy is not used and is available for creating new symbols. This excess of libido is due to the failure of the personality system to equalize completely the differences in the energy intensities. For example, if an energy value is transferred from the persona to the anima, and the anima fails to incorporate the full value of the energy, there will be some energy left over. It is this excess energy that is available for canalizing or creating new symbols (analogies). These symbols will lead us to new activities, interests, discoveries, and patterns of life. Excess libido has enabled man to advance from being a creature of natural instincts, through the stage of superstition and magic, to the modern era of science, technology, and art. Sometimes, of course, the excess of energy is used for destructive and even diabolical ends. "Acts of will" can be used to destroy as well as to create.

VIII. SUMMARY

The psyche is a relatively closed energy system. It derives its *energy* (libido) primarily from experiences which enter the psyche by way of the sense organs. A secondary source is instinctual energy, but most of this energy is used for purely instinctual or natural life activities. The amount of energy invested in an element of the psyche is called its *value*. The intensity of a value can be estimated relatively, but it cannot be measured absolutely.

The distribution of energy throughout the psyche is determined by two principles. The principle of *equivalence* states that when energy is lost from one psychic component an equivalent amount of energy will appear in another component or components. The principle of *en-*

tropy states that energy will tend to move from a component of high value to one of low value until the two values are equalized.

Libido can flow in either of two directions, *progressively* toward adapting to external situations, and *regressively* toward activating unconscious material. Instinctual energy can be diverted into a new activity when it is like (analogous to or symbolic of) the instinctual activity. This is called *canalization*.

The key concepts in Jungian psychodynamics are psychic energy or libido, value, equivalence, entropy, progression and regression, and canalization.

REFERENCE

JUNG, C. G. *Collected Works.* Princeton, N. J.: Princeton University Press.
   Vol. 8. *The Structure and Dynamics of the Psyche.*

CHAPTER FOUR

The Development
of Personality

There are two reasons why a psychotherapist needs to have a firm grasp of the developmental processes in personality. One reason is that patients who are seen by the therapist are ordinarily drawn from all ages, from children to old people. The psychic state of a young person is in a different stage of development from that of an older person. Consequently, the problems which a young person brings to the therapist are not the same problems that an older person needs help with. The problems of a person in the first half of life pertain to instinctual adaptations, and those in the second half of life pertain to adaptations to his own being.

The second reason is that psychotherapy, if it is to be effective, has to produce growth in the patient. An awareness of what it means to grow, the nature of the growth processes, and how to activate growth is essential knowledge for the therapist.

Out of his vast experience, Jung generated a number of basic concepts referring to the development of personality. It is these concepts that we will discuss in the present chapter.

I. INDIVIDUATION

The individual begins his life in a state of undifferentiated wholeness. Then, just as a seed grows into a plant, the individual develops into a fully differentiated, balanced, and unified personality. That, at least, is the direction development takes, although the goal of complete differentiation, balance, and unity is rarely if ever reached, except, as Jung observes, by a Jesus or a Buddha. This striving for self-realization or consummate selfhood is archetypal, that is to say, inborn. No one can avoid the powerful influence of this unity archetype, although what course its expression may take and how successful one may be in realizing the aim varies from person to person.

Jung's key developmental concept is *individuation*. The various systems of the personality described in Chapter Two are said to become more and more individuated during one's life. This means not only that each system becomes differentiated from every other system but more importantly that each system becomes differentiated within itself. From a simple structure it grows into a complex structure, just as a larva develops into a butterfly. Complexity means that the structure is capable of expressing itself in a variety of ways. For example, the undeveloped ego has a few simple ways of being conscious; as it becomes individuated its repertoire of conscious acts becomes greatly expanded. The individuated ego is capable of making fine discriminations among its perceptions of the world; it apprehends subtle relationships among ideas, and probes deeper into the meaning of objective phenomena.

In a similar manner, the persona, anima, shadow, and the other archetypes of the collective unconscious and the complexes of the personal unconscious express themselves in more subtle and intricate ways as they become individuated. When Jung asserts that man is constantly searching for better symbols he means that increasing individuation demands more elaborate and refined outlets. For instance, simple nursery rhymes and games satisfy children, but they do not satisfy the individuated adult. He needs the more complex symbolism of religion, literature, the arts, and social institutions.

Individuation is an autonomous, inborn process, which means that it does not require external stimulation in order to come into existence. The personality of an individual is destined to individuate just as surely as the body is destined to grow. But just as the body needs proper food and exercise for healthy growth, so the personality needs proper experiences and education for healthy individuation. And just as the body can become stunted, deformed, and sickly as a result of an inadequate diet or lack of exercise, so the personality can be deformed by deficiencies in its experiences and education. As Jung points out, for example, the modern world provides inadequate opportunities for the shadow archetype to become individuated. Expressions of the animal instincts by the child are commonly punished by his parents. Punishment does not lead to a disappearance of the shadow archetype—nothing can do that—but to its repression. It returns to the unconscious sphere of personality, where it remains in a primitive, undifferentiated state. Then when it breaks through the barrier of repression—as it is bound to do from time to time—the shadow manifests itself in sinister, pathological ways. The savage sadism of modern warfare and the crude obscenities of pornography exemplify the actions of an undifferentiated shadow.

Only by becoming conscious can a system of personality proceed to individuate. Presumably, this is, or should be, the ultimate goal of education, to make conscious that which is unconscious. Education, as the etymology of the word indicates, is a drawing out from the person of something that is already there in a nascent state, and not the filling up of an empty container with knowledge.

For healthy development, all facets of the personality must be given an equal opportunity to become individuated. For if one part of the personality is neglected, this neglected part will find abnormal ways of expressing itself. The inflation of a system will create a lopsided personality. Suppose that the environment in which a child is raised emphasizes conventional standards of conduct. The child is supposed to pretend to like something when he does not, and to not like something when he does. He is taught to think and act in accordance with a traditional set of values. In Jungian language, he develops an inflated persona. The conscious behavior of such a person is characterized by a lack of zest, vitality, and spontaneity. He is nothing but a mask, a puppet of society.

Psychotherapy is primarily an individuation process. In *Psychology and Alchemy* Jung explores the course of individuation as expressed in the dreams and visions of a patient. In another work entitled "A Study in the Process of Individuation" (Vol. 9i), individuation is expressed through a series of watercolors made by a middle-aged woman undergoing treatment by Jung. The paintings are in the form of mandalas, that is, circular shapes (representing the psyche) which contains intricately balanced designs. An analysis of the successive designs tells the story of the individuation process in this woman. Jung observes that patients often acknowledge the soothing effects of drawing mandala figures. The reader will find fifty-three mandala figures reproduced in Jung's article "Concerning Mandala Symbolism" (Vol. 9i).

II. TRANSCENDENCE AND INTEGRATION

The integration of personality is one of the prominent themes in Jungian psychology. How is this integration to be accomplished when the personality is made up of so many different systems, some of which, at least, seem to be in conflict with each other? For example, it is difficult to see how the shadow and the persona could ever become parts of an integrated whole.

The first step toward integration is, as we have just seen, individuation of *all* aspects of personality. The second stage is controlled by what Jung calls the *transcendent function*. This function is endowed with the capability of uniting all of the opposing trends in personality and of working toward the goal of wholeness. The aim of the transcendent function, Jung writes, is "the realization, in all of its aspects, of the personality originally hidden away in the embryonic germplasm; the production and unfolding of the original potential wholeness." The transcendent function is the means by which the unity or self archetype is realized. Like the process of individuation, the transcendent function is inherent in the person.

We have said that individuation and integration are separate steps. Actually, they go hand in hand so that differentiation and unification are coexisting processes in the development of personality. Together they produce the ultimate achievement of a completely realized selfhood.

Let us illustrate transcendence by considering the integration of the anima with the masculine side of man's personality. At the same time that each of these components is being permitted to individuate by being expressed (rather than repressed) in conscious acts, they are also tending to form an amalgam. That is, each conscious act comes to express both sides of a man's nature. Instead of opposition or separation, there is a harmonious blend. The man who has integrated his anima with his maleness is *not* one whose behavior is sometimes in the masculine mode and sometimes in the feminine mode. He is *not* part man and part woman. Rather, a true synthesis between opposites has been achieved so that it may be said transcendence has abolished gender except in a biological sense.

Of course, perfect selfhood is only an ideal toward which the personality is motivated; rarely, if ever, is it achieved.

One must consider, therefore, the factors that obstruct the realization of a completely individuated and integrated personality. It is possible, Jung believed, that heredity may underlie a lopsided personality. A person may be born with a strong disposition to be extraverted or introverted; he may be destined to become a feeling type rather than a thinking type; his anima or his shadow may be strong or weak by nature. The influence of heredity on personality is a subject of which we have little knowledge.

The other great influence on the development of personality is, of course, the environment. Jung, like all other great psychologists, was a social critic. That is, he identified and analyzed the factors in the environment that he felt were responsible for hindering or deforming development. The environment, it is true, can also aid development. It does so when it nourishes the inherent qualities of the individual or helps to bring them into balance. It hinders growth when it deprives the person of the necessary nutriments or when it provides the wrong supplies.

A. THE ROLE OF THE PARENTS   Virtually every psychologist who has studied the development of personality emphasizes the self-evident proposition that the parents of a child play an extremely important role in the development of the child's character. They (the parents) are blamed for the child's faults and praised, although not as frequently, for the child's virtues. Of course Jung recognizes this self-evident truth.

However, he puts forth some fairly novel ideas about

the effects of parental behavior on the child's personality. In the first place, the child has no separate identity during the early years of his life; his psyche is a reflection of the parents' psyches. Therefore, the child's psyche is bound to reflect any psychic disturbances in the parents. Consequently, psychotherapy for children consists for the most part of analyzing the parents. Jung even says that the child's dreams are not so much his own as those of his parents. In one case he describes, a father was analyzed through the dreams of his young son. The son's dreams were a mirror of the state of the father's psyche at the time.

When the child goes to school, his identity with his parents begins to weaken and he begins to develop his own individuality. There is, of course, the danger that the parents will continue to dominate the child by overprotecting him, by making decisions for him, and by preventing him from having a wide range of experiences. Under such circumstances, the child's individuation will be hampered.

It will also be hampered if either or both of the parents try to force their own psychic constitutions on the child, or if either of them tries to compensate for his own psychic deficiencies by encouraging the child to overdevelop in his personality these deficiencies of the parent. For example, introverted parents may want their children to be like them or they may want them to be extraverts. In either case, the child will suffer imbalances in his own personality. Should he be the battleground between a mother and a father who are trying to project on him different psychic structures, the result will be even more harmful.

The mother's role is different from that of the father's. The child's experiences with the mother determines the way in which his *anima* develops, whereas his experiences with the father determines the way in which his *shadow* develops. The reverse is true for a girl. Both parents are instrumental in forming the child's *persona*.

B. THE INFLUENCE OF EDUCATION   As pointed out in Chapter One, Jung had a number of unpleasant experiences during his schooling, particularly with teachers who did not understand him. He thought much of the subject matter he was supposed to learn was boring. Perhaps remembering his own schooling, Jung in a number of talks to educators stressed the need to understand psychic development during childhood and adolescence. He felt that the influence of the teacher on the personality development of his pupils was of equal importance to his influence on their intellectual and scholastic accomplishments. Consequently, the education of teachers should include psychological subjects, and even more important, it should emphasize the prospective teacher's need to know his own personality. Otherwise, when he went into the classroom he would carry his own complexes and problems with him and project them on his pupils. Just as children reflect the psychic problems of their parents, so pupils reflect the psychic problems of their teachers. Since it would be unrealistic to expect all teachers to undergo analytical therapy, Jung urged them to keep a record of their dreams and try to learn something about themselves from these nocturnal eruptions of the unconscious.

There was no question in Jung's mind that educators were the most potent influences on the child's individuation, and were even more potent than the parents. Teachers are or should be trained to bring into the conscious ego of the student that which is unconscious. They also expand his consciousness by providing him with a wealth of new experiences and with symbols that will attract energy away from the instincts. Teachers are in a position to recognize disharmonies in a child's personality and to help him strengthen the weaker elements. The overdeveloped thinking-type pupil can be encouraged to express the undifferentiated feeling function, the introverted pupil can be encouraged to develop his weak extraversion. It is especially important for women teachers to be aware of the state of a boy's anima and for men teachers to be aware of the state of a girl's animus. The most important function of the teacher, however, is to recognize the individuality of each of his pupils and to foster the balanced development of this individuality.

C. OTHER INFLUENCES   The larger society in which the individual lives also has an impact on the integration of his personality. Jung points out that fashions change with respect to what personality types are preferred. In one period of history, feeling may be favored; in another, thinking may be the popular function. The anima may be repressed at one time and encouraged at another. Imbalances in personality often result from these changing fashions. In the late 1960's the anima in males and the animus in females began to individuate with greater acceleration. At the same time the persona started to undergo a deflation, and the expansion of consciousness became an aim of the generation born during the postwar years.

Jung also says that different cultures may favor different personality types. In the Far East, for example, introversion and intuition are favored, whereas in the West extraversion and thinking are valued.

Individuation is not a process that operates within the individual exclusively. It also operates over generations of mankind and between civilized and primitive man. Modern man is more individuated than ancient man, and civilized man is more individuated than primitive man. What this means in practical terms is that old forms of thought and behavior cannot satisfy the personality requirements of modern man. In Jung's terms, modern man needs more complex symbols by which to express his higher level of individuation. The Renaissance was a period of tremendous change in which many new symbols were created. What is needed today, Jung avers, is another Renaissance of symbolism. Lacking viable symbols, what occurs is the unleashing of repressed, undeveloped archetypes in primitive self-destructive acts.

At one time religion played a much larger role than it does today in helping the individual to individuate and integrate his personality. It did so by providing him with powerful symbols for the realization of selfhood. As religious institutions became more involved with secular issues such as social reform, and paid less attention to maintaining the viability of archetypal symbols, the value of religion for the individual's psychic development diminished. Jung wrote extensively on psychology and religion, and his views have had a strong influence on some clergymen. One result has been the growth of pastoral counseling, a field in which clergymen trained in analytical psychology offer counseling within a religious framework. The recent surge of interest, especially among young people, in various types of religious experiences may be due, in part, to the writings of Jung.

III. REGRESSION

We had occasion to discuss the concept of regression in the last chapter. In the context of dynamics, regression refers to the backward flow of libido. In this chapter, regression will be discussed in terms of development.

Development may follow either a progressive, forward direction or a regressive, backward direction. By progression is meant that the conscious ego is harmonizing the reality of the environment with the needs of the whole psyche. When this harmony is broken by an environmental frustration or deprivation, the libido is withdrawn from the extraverted values of the environment and invests itself in the introverted values of the unconscious. This withdrawing into one's self is what Jung calls *regression*. Regression can be useful to adjustment when the frustrated person finds the solution to his problem in the unconscious. The unconscious, it will be recalled, contains the knowledge and wisdom of one's individual and racial past. Withdrawing from the bustle of the world and indulging in quiet meditation, from time to time, is highly recommended by Jung as a means of achieving or maintaining harmony and integration. Many creative people engage in periodic retreats in order to revitalize themselves by partaking of the vast resources of the unconscious. Jung himself practiced what he preached by retreating to his Bollingen house.

Of course, we retreat into sleep every night. This is a time when the mind is cut off almost completely from the external world and turns in upon itself and produces dreams. This nightly regression into the unconscious is capable of providing a person with useful information about the nature of the obstacles that impede development, and suggestions as to how these obstacles may be overcome. Unfortunately, people do not pay much attention to their dreams, which for Jung are a rich source of psychic wisdom. There is scarcely one of his writings in which the use of dream analysis for understanding the archetypal basis of personality is not illustrated. We shall have more to say about Jung's views on dreams in Chapter Six.

The interaction of progression and regression in development may be illustrated by the following example. An individual overdevelops his persona to such a degree that he is little more than a robot acting in conformity with social convention and tradition. As a consequence, he becomes listless, bored, irritable, dissatisfied, and depressed. Finally, he feels the need of getting away from his mundane life, and he goes off by himself. He sheds the rigid mask of conformity and discovers the hidden riches in the unconscious. He returns to his everyday life refreshed and invigorated, more of a spontaneous, creative person and less of a puppet of the environment. Legends of rebirth express in mythical terms the benefits of regression.

Unfortunately, the foregoing example is idealized. Most people who find themselves imprisoned by convention resort to diversions such as drinking, gambling, fighting, and sensuality, from which they learn nothing.

IV. STAGES OF LIFE

Although development is continuous throughout one's lifetime, several important transitions in development take place, and so one may speak of *stages of life*. Instead of the seven stages described by Shakespeare, Jung recognizes four.

A. CHILDHOOD   This stage begins at birth and lasts until puberty or sexual maturity. At birth and for several years thereafter, there are virtually no problems for the child. Problems require a conscious ego, which the young child does not have. He is conscious, to be sure, but there is little or no organization in his perceptions, and his conscious memory is very transient. Consequently, there is no continuity of consciousness and no sense of personal identity. During these early years when whatever psychic life he has is governed by instinct, the child is entirely dependent upon his parents and lives enclosed in a psychic atmosphere provided by them. His behavior is anarchic, lacking order and control, and it is chaotic. Some order is provided by the instincts: he gets hungry and thirsty periodically, eliminates when his bladder or bowels are full, and sleeps when tired. But most of the order in his life has to be programmed for him by the parents.

Later during this stage, the ego will begin to form, partly as a consequence of the lengthening of memory, and partly because an ego-complex around which perceptions connected with a sense of personal identity—an I-ness—is energized and individuated. The child starts to speak of himself in the first person. When he enters school, he begins to emerge from the parental enclosure or psychic womb.

B. YOUTH AND YOUNG ADULTHOOD   This stage is announced by the physiological changes that occur during puberty. "The physiological change is attended by a psychic revolution" (Vol. 8, p. 391). Jung referred to it as "psychic birth" because the psyche begins to take its own shape. The psychic revolution becomes quite apparent when adolescents assert themselves with a great deal of force and excitement. During the adolescent years—often called the unbearable age, unbearable for parents and young person alike—the psyche is burdened with problems, decisions, and the necessity for making many different kinds of adaptations to social life. Many of these problems originate when the individual is confronted with the demands of life that abruptly put an end to the childish fantasies.

If the individual is adequately prepared, adjusted, and aware, the transition from childhood activities to a vocation can be accomplished without too much difficulty. However, if he adheres to the illusions of childhood and fails to recognize reality, he will most certainly encounter a multitude of problems.

Everyone walks into the life of responsibility with certain expectations, and sometimes these expectations collapse. Quite often they collapse because they do not apply to the situation which confronts the individual. For example, if a young man spends his youth planning to be an airplane pilot, and then it is discovered that his vision is inadequate for this type of vocation, his expectations will be dashed. These expectations cannot very easily be applied to another vocation. Other reasons why expectations can collapse is that a person can exaggerate his expectations, be overly optimistic or have a pessimistic attitude, or underestimate the problems he may encounter.

Not all of the problems which occur during the second stage are related to external affairs, such as a vocation or getting married. The problems may just as often be inner, psychic difficulties. Very often, Jung notes, it is the disturbance of psychic equilibrium caused by the sexual instinct; equally often it is a feeling of inferiority which stems from extreme sensitivity and insecurity.

The innumerable problems of youth usually have one feature in common, and that is the clinging to a childhood level of consciousness. Some deep feeling within us (a child archteype) prefers to remain a child instead of growing up.

The tasks confronting the person in the second stage of life have more to do with extraverted values. He has to make his place in the world. For this reason, the strengthening of will is of the utmost importance. A young man or young woman must have sufficient will to be efficient in making decisions, to be able to overcome the innumerable barriers that he will face, and to achieve the material satisfactions that he desires for himself and for his family.

C. MIDDLE AGE   The second stage ends somewhere between the ages of 35 and 40. By this age, a person has usually adapted himself more or less successfully to the external environment. He has established himself in a vocation, married and had children, and become an active participant in community and civic affairs. Except for occasional frustrations, disappointments, and discontents, it might be expected that a middle-aged person would live out the second half of his life in a relatively settled state.

This is not the case, however. The second half of life presents problems of adaptation which are peculiar to it and for which the person is not prepared. His main task during the third stage is to recenter his life around a new set of values. Energy that was formerly used for external adaptations must be directed into these new values.

What is the nature of these values that demand to be recognized after the age of 35? Jung says they are spiritual values. These spiritual values have always been in the psyche in a latent condition but had to be neglected because of the inflation of extraverted, materialistic interests during the youthful years. The necessity to direct psychic energy from the old channels established during the second stage into new channels is one of the greatest challenges of life. It is a challenge that many people cannot meet successfully and that may even wreck their lives.

Psychologists have paid little attention to this crucial period, preferring to concentrate their investigations on infancy, childhood, adolescence, and old age. Jung is one of the few psychologists who tried to understand the psychology of the middle years. He says he was forced to think about this problem because so many of his patients—fully two-thirds of them—were in this third stage. One wonders also whether Jung's own experiences in making the transition did not contribute to his interest in this period. Jung was 36 years old when he wrote *Symbols of Transformation*, a book that signaled his break with Freud and laid the foundation for all of his future work and thought. He also notes in his autobiography that he went through a fallow period following the publication of this book, a period, we may surmise, when new values were being incubated.

Many of Jung's patients were men and women of the highest accomplishments who were eminently successful in their vocations and enjoyed an enviable position in society. They were often highly creative, intelligent individuals. Why did they feel the need to consult Jung? Because, as they confessed to him in the privacy of his consulting room, life had lost not only its zest and sense of adventure, which might be understandable considering their age, but also its meaning. Things which had formerly been extremely important to them were no longer important. Their lives seemed empty and meaningless. They felt depressed.

Jung discovered the reason for their depressive attitude. The energy that had been invested in interests which were necessary for attaining a position in society had been withdrawn from these interests, because their aims had been realized. Loss of value creates a vacuum in the personality.

What is the cure? The obvious answer is that new values have to arise which will take the place of the outworn values and fill the vacuum. Just any interests will not do, however. They have to be values that will broaden the horizons of the person beyond purely materialistic considerations. These horizons are spiritual and cultural. It is a time for self-realization through contemplation and meditation rather than activity. As Jung states the situation, "It is of the greatest importance for the young person, who is still unadapted and has as yet achieved nothing, to shape his conscious ego as effectively as possible, that is, to educate his will. . . . It is otherwise with a person in the second half of life who no longer needs to educate his conscious will, but who, to understand the meaning of his individual life, needs to experience his own inner being" (Vol. 16, p. 50).

D. OLD AGE   This is the period of extreme old age, and holds little interest for Jung. In one respect, old age is like childhood; the person is submerged in the unconscious and did not flinch from considering the question of a hereafter. who emerges into consciousness, the aged individual sinks into the unconscious and finally vanishes within it.

Does human personality cease to exist when the body dies? Is there a life after death? It may seem strange and perverse for a psychologist to raise such questions. Jung did not flinch from considering the question of a hereafter. He knew that a belief which was held by so many people in the world, which was a primary element in many religions, and which was the theme of numerous myths and dreams should not be dismissed contemptuously as mere superstition. There must be some basis in the unconscious for this belief. One possibility is that the idea of a life after death represents another stage in the individuation of the psyche. Psychic life, it is conjectured, goes on after physical death because the psyche has not attained complete self-realization.

V. SUMMARY

The growth of personality consists of two interwoven strands: *individuation* of the various structures that make up the total psyche, and *integration* of these structures into a unified whole (selfhood). These growth processes are influenced either positively or negatively by a number of conditions, including heredity, the child's experiences with his parents, education, religion, society, and age. There is a radical change in development during the middle years of life. This consists of a transition from adaptations to the external world to adaptations to one's inner being.

REFERENCES

JUNG, C. G. *Collected Works*. Princeton, N. J.: Princeton University Press.
    Vol. 8. *The Structure and Dynamics of the Psyche.*
    Vol. 9i. *The Archetypes and the Collective Unconscious.*
    Vol. 12. *Psychology and Alchemy.*
    Vol. 16. *The Practice of Psychotherapy.*
    Vol. 17. *The Development of Personality.*

CHAPTER FIVE

Psychological Types

In 1921, Jung published the results of his studies of psychological types. This book, he wrote in the foreword, is "the fruit of nearly twenty years' work in the domain of practical psychology. It grew gradually in my thoughts, taking shape from the countless impressions and experiences of a psychiatrist in the treatment of nervous illnesses, from intercourse with men and women of all social levels, from my personal dealings with friend and foe alike, and finally from a critique of my own psychological peculiarity" (Vol. 6, p. xi).

What Jung accomplished in *Psychological Types* was of twofold importance: he identified and described a number of *basic* psychological processes, and he showed how these processes merged in various combinations to determine an individual's character. He set out to transform a general psychology of universal laws and processes into an individual psychology that described the unique characteristics and behavior of a specific person. The result was, as Jung said, a very practical psychology. "It was one of the greatest experiences of my life to discover how enormously different people's psyches are" (Vol. 10, p. 137).

We shall show how this application of abstract concepts to individual cases was accomplished by presenting the basic attitudes and functions first, followed by a description of the types of individuals that result from various combinations of these attitudes and functions in varying proportions. The types, it should be understood, are categories into which people with similar but not necessarily identical characteristics are placed. Even within the same category, no two individuals personality patterns are exactly alike.

I. THE ATTITUDES

Jung's well-known distinction between the basic attitudes of extraversion and introversion constitutes one dimension for his system of classification. In order to understand the full significance of these key terms, it is necessary to distinguish between two other words, *objective* and *subjective*. *Objective* refers to the world that lies outside of and surrounds the person; a world of people and things, of customs and conventions, of political, economic, and social institutions, and of physical conditions. This objective world is referred to as the environment, the surroundings, or external reality. *Subjective* designates the inner and private world of the psyche. It is private because it is not directly observable by outsiders. In fact, it is so private that it is not even always directly accessible to the conscious mind. Access to these unconscious psychic elements is often attainable only through assistance from a psychotherapist or from the analysis of one's dreams.

In extraversion, psychic energy (libido) is channeled into representations of the objective external world, and invests itself in perceptions, thoughts, and feelings about objects, people and animals, and other environmental circumstances and conditions. In introversion, libido flows toward subjective psychic structures and processes. Extraversion is an objective attitude; introversion is a subjective attitude.

These two attitudes are mutually exclusive; they cannot coexist simultaneously in consciousness, although they can and do alternate with one another. A person may be extraverted on some occasions and introverted on other occasions. However, one attitude usually predominates in a given individual during his lifetime. If the objective orientation predominates, the person is called an *extravert*, whereas if the subjective orientation is ascendant, he is called an *introvert*.

The introvert is interested in exploring and analyzing his inner world; he is introspective, withdrawn, and very much preoccupied by his own internal affairs. He may appear to others as being aloof, unsocial, and reserved. The extravert is preoccupied by his interactions with people and things. He appears to be more active and outgoing, and to take an interest in things around him.

Ascendancy of one attitude over the other is a matter of degree. A person is more or less extraverted or introverted; he is not totally the one or totally the other. "We call a mode of behavior extraverted only when the mechanism of extraversion predominates" (Vol. 6, p. 575).

Moreover, the distinction is blurred by the presence in the unconscious of the opposite attitude from the attitude which is expressed in consciousness. The conscious extravert is an introvert in his unconscious, and the conscious introvert is an extravert in his unconscious. This is an instance of the compensatory role that the unconscious plays in the psyche.

It is to be noted that an attitude has different characteristics when it is unconscious from those which it has when it is conscious. A conscious extravert or introvert expresses his extraversion or introversion directly by his conscious behavior. This behavior can be readily observed by others as being extraverted or introverted. We all recognize a person who is withdrawn, abstracted, and disengaged from the external world. He appears to be lost in his own thoughts. The compensatory unconscious attitude cannot express itself openly because it is repressed. It does, however, influence behavior indirectly, as when a person behaves in a way that is incongruous or bizarre for him. We are astonished, for example, when an extraverted person suddenly becomes moody, contrary, or unsocial. "What's eating him?" we ask. The answer is: his unconscious. He is temporarily in the grip of his repressed introversion.

Unconscious processes are not as well developed and differentiated as conscious ones are, so that the effect of the repressed attitude has a tendency to make behavior more primitive and crude. An extreme example of this is the introvert who for no reason at all suddenly runs amok. Furthermore, according to Jung's compensatory theory of dreams, an extravert is an introvert in his dream life, and an introvert becomes an extravert when he falls asleep.

II. THE FUNCTIONS

Of equal importance to the attitudes in Jung's typology are the psychological *functions*, of which there are four:

thinking, feeling, sensation, and intuition. *Thinking* consists of connecting ideas with each other in order to arrive at a general concept or a solution to a problem. It is an intellectual function that seeks to understand things.

Feeling is an evaluative function; it either accepts or rejects an idea on the basis of whether the idea arouses a pleasant or unpleasant feeling.

Thinking and feeling are said to be *rational* functions because they both require an act of judgment. In thinking, one makes judgments as to whether there is a true connection between two or more ideas. In feeling, one makes judgments as to whether an idea is pleasing or distasteful, beautiful or ugly, exciting or dull.

Sensation is sense perception which comprises all conscious experiences produced by stimulation of the sense organs—sights, sounds, smells, tastes, and touch as well as sensations originating inside the body. *Intuition* is like sensation in being an experience which is immediately given rather than produced as a result of thought or feeling. No judgment is necessary. Intuition differs from sensation because the person who has an intuition does not know where it came from or how it originated. It appears "out of the blue." Sensation can always be accounted for by pointing to the source of the stimulation. "I have a toothache." "I see a whale." But when a person has an intuition or hunch that something is going to happen and is asked how he knows, he can only reply, "I feel it in my bones" or "I just *know*." Intuition is sometimes called the sixth sense, or extrasensory perception.

Sensation and intuition are said to be *irrational* functions because they require no reason. They are mental states that evolve from the flux of stimuli acting upon the individual. This flux lacks direction or intentionality; it has no aim as thinking and feeling do. What one senses is contingent upon the stimuli that are present. What one feels in one's bones depends upon unknown stimuli. Jung does not mean by irrational that which is contrary to reason. Sensation and intuition simply have nothing to do with reason. They are nonrational and nonjudgmental.

Jung defined the four functions very succinctly, as follows: "These four functional types correspond to the obvious means by which consciousness obtains its orientation to experience. *Sensation* (i.e. sense perception) tells us that something exists; *thinking* tells you what it is; *feeling* tells you whether it is agreeable or not; and *intuition* tells you whence it comes and where it is going" (*Man and His Symbols*, 1964, p. 61).

Since the characteristics of the functions differ depending on whether they are combined with extraversion or introversion, it is necessary to discuss the eight possible combinations separately.

III. COMBINATIONS OF ATTITUDES AND FUNCTIONS

Extraverted thinking utilizes information supplied to the brain by stimulation of the sense organs. The object which activates the thinking process is something that exists in the external world. One tries to explain how a seed germinates and grows into a plant, or why water turns into steam when heated to a certain temperature, or how a language is learned. Jung observes that many people would consider this to be the only type of thinking possible. This is not so, he says. There is also *introverted thinking,* which consists of thinking subjectively. Instead of thinking thoughts originating exclusively from the external world, a person also thinks about the inner mental world. One might say the introverted thinker is interested in ideas for their own sake. He may search the external world for facts to confirm his ideas. In science, this is called deductive thinking as contrasted with inductive thinking, in which ideas or hypotheses or concepts grow out of and are based upon factual information. Or the person may continue to ruminate about his ideas, disregarding whether they have any relevance to the external world.

The extraverted thinker is more pragmatic or practical. He is a problem solver.

Extraverted feeling is governed by external or objective criteria. One feels, for instance, that something is beautiful or ugly because either it does or does not meet traditional established esthetic standards. For that reason, extraverted feeling tends to be conventional and conservative. Like introverted thinking, *introverted feeling* is aroused by internal or subjective conditions, especially primordial images arising out of archetypes. Since these images are both thoughts and feelings, the predominance of the former results in introverted thinking, whereas the predominance of the latter results in introverted feeling. Introverted feeling tends to be original, unusual, creative, and sometimes bizarre because it deviates from convention.

In *extraverted sensation*, sensations are determined by the nature of the objective reality that confronts the person; in *introverted sensation*, sensations are determined by the subjective reality at a particular time. In the one case, perceptions represent objects directly; they are facts in the external world. In the other case, perceptions are heavily influenced by psychic states; they seem to emerge from somewhere within the psyche.

Extraverted intuition seeks to discover the possibilities of every objective situation, and is continuously looking for new possibilities in external objects. *Introverted intuition* searches out the possibilities of mental phenomena, especially images arising from archetypes. Extraverted intuition moves from object to object; introverted intuition moves from image to image.

Let us now consider how these combinations of the attitudes and functions consciously express themselves in the behavioral patterns of individuals. The individual expression constitutes Jung's typology, which consists of eight types of people. We will describe some extreme cases of the various types, as Jung does, but it is to be understood that there are many gradations within each type.

IV. TYPES OF INDIVIDUALS

A. EXTRAVERTED THINKING TYPE   This type of man elevates objective thinking into the ruling passion of his life. He is typified by the scientist who devotes his energy to learning as much as he can about the objective world. His goals are understanding natural phenomena, the discovery of natural laws, and theoretical formulations. The most developed type of extraverted thinker is a Darwin or an Einstein. The extraverted thinker tends to repress the feeling side of his nature, and so he may appear to others as being impersonal, or even cold and haughty.

If the repression is too strict, feeling is forced to find devious and sometimes abnormal ways of affecting his character. He may become autocratic, bigoted, vain, superstitious, and impervious to criticism. Lacking feeling, the quality of his thinking tends to become sterile and impoverished. The extreme case is the "mad scientist" or the Dr. Jekyll who periodically turns into a psychopathic monster.

B. INTRODUCED THINKING TYPE This type is inward-directed in his thinking. He is exemplified by the philosopher or existential psychologist who seeks to understand the reality of his own being. In extreme cases, the result of his explorations may bear little relation to reality. He may eventually break his ties with reality and become schizophrenic. He shares many of the same character traits with his extraverted counterpart, and for the same reason, namely, because he has to protect himself from feelings which have been repressed into the unconscious. He appears to be emotionless and distant because he does not value people. He wants to be left alone to pursue his own thoughts. He is not particularly concerned about having his ideas accepted by others, although he may have a few devoted followers of the same type that he is. He is inclined to be stubborn, headstrong, inconsiderate, arrogant, prickly, unapproachable, and standoffish. With the intensification of this type, the thinking becomes more subject to abnormal and quixotic influences from the repressed feeling function.

C. EXTRAVERTED FEELING TYPE This type, which Jung observes is more frequently found in women, subordinates thinking to feeling. People of this type are apt to be capricious because their feelings change as frequently as the situation changes. Even a slight variance in the situation may cause a change in their feelings. They are gushy, emotional, ostentatious, and moody. They form strong attachments to people, but these attachments are transitory, and love easily turns into hate. Their feelings are fairly conventional, and they readily participate in all the latest fads and fashions. When the thinking function is firmly repressed, the thought processes of the extraverted feeling type are primitive and undeveloped.

D. INTROVERTED FEELING TYPE   This type is also more commonly found among women. Unlike their extraverted sisters, who parade their emotions, introverted feeling persons keep their feelings hidden from the world. They tend to be silent, inaccessible, indifferent, and inscrutable. They often have an air of melancholy or depression. But they can also give the impression of having inner harmony, repose, and self-sufficiency. They often seem to others to have a mysterious power or charisma. They are people of whom it is said, "Still waters run deep." Actually, they do have very deep and intense feelings which sometimes erupt in emotional storms, to the astonishment of their relatives and friends.

E. EXTRAVERTED SENSATION TYPE   People of this type, mainly men, take an interest in accumulating facts about the external world. They are realistic, practical, and hardheaded but they are not particularly concerned about what things mean. They accept the world as it is without giving it much thought or foresight. But they can also be sensual, pleasure-loving, and thrill-seeking. Their feelings are shallow. They live simply for the sensations they can derive from life. Extreme cases become crude sensualists or pretentious esthetes. Due to their sensual orientation they are susceptible to addictions of various kinds, perversions, and compulsions.

F. INTROVERTED SENSATION TYPE   Like all introverts, the introverted sensation type stands aloof from external objects, immersing himself in his own psychic sensations. He considers the world to be banal and uninteresting in comparison with his inner sensations. He has difficulty expressing himself except through art, but what he produces tends to be devoid of any significance. To others he may appear to be calm, passive, and self-controlled, when actually he is not very interesting because he is deficient in thought and feeling.

G. EXTRAVERTED INTUITIVE TYPE   People of this type, commonly women, are characterized by flightiness and instability; they jump from situation to situation to discover new possibilities in the external world. They are always looking for new worlds to conquer before they have conquered old ones. Because they are deficient in the thinking function, they cannot diligently pursue their intuitions for very long but must jump to new intuitions. They can render exceptional service as promoters of new enterprises and causes, but they cannot maintain an interest in them. Routine activities bore them; novelty is their life's sustenance. They tend to fritter away their lives on a succession of intuitions. They are not dependable friends, although they enter into each new relationship with great zest for the possibilities it holds. As a consequence they unwittingly hurt people by their lack of sustained interest. They take up numerous hobbies but soon get bored with them, and they have difficulty keeping a job.

H. INTRODUCTED INTUITIVE TYPE   The artist is a representative of this type, but it also contains dreamers, prophets, visionaries, and cranks. An introverted intuitive person is often regarded as an enigma by his friends, and as a misunderstood genius by himself. Since he is not in touch with external reality or with conventions, he is unable to communicate effectively with others, even with those of the same type. He is isolated in a world of primordial images whose meaning he does not understand. Like his extraverted counterpart, he jumps from image to image looking for new possibilities in them but never really develops any of his intuitions. Since he is unable to sustain an interest in an image, he cannot, as the introverted thinker does, make any profound contribution to an understanding of psychic processes. He can, however, have brilliant intuitions which others may then build upon and develop.

This concludes our presentation of the eight classes of character types. Again we remind the reader that the examples chosen for each type represent extreme cases. By extreme cases we mean the conscious attitude is highly *developed*, and its repressed counterpart in the unconscious is virtually *undeveloped*. Thus the conscious attitude becomes extreme because the unconscious counterpart provides no resistance or balancing effect, as it would in more normal cases. These character descriptions read more like caricatures than like characters.

It is much more typical for a person to be both extraverted *and* introverted, and to make use of all the functions, in varying proportions. Ordinarily, however, a person will be more extraverted than introverted or vice versa. Rarely will the two attitudes be in perfect balance. A person will also tend to use one function more than the other three. Jung calls this the *principal function.* In addition, there is an *auxiliary function.* The auxiliary function renders its service to the principal function; it has no independence of its own. Consequently, it cannot stand in opposition to the principal function. Since thinking and feeling are both rational functions they tend to oppose each other. Neither of them can be auxiliary for the other. The same is true of the irrational functions of sensation and intuition. Sensation or intuition can be an auxiliary function for thinking or feeling and vice versa. Suppose, for example, that a person's principal function is thinking. He can then use information obtained from sensation as an accessory aid to thinking. Intuition can serve equally well as an auxiliary function to thinking by providing hunches and insights that can then be thought through. In fact, some of the most brilliant people utilize the combination of thinking and intuition. The same is true of the pairing of feeling with intuition. The former (combination of thinking and intuition) is apt to be a great scientist or philosopher, the latter a great artist. Ideally, it would be advantageous to a person to have the attitudes and functions equally developed and equally available for use, but this is not the way it works out. There will always be inequities among the various components of the psyche even though the psyche as a whole strives for harmony and balance.

Each individual has his own unique pattern of attitudes and functions, although in no case are any of the attitudes or functions missing. If they do not exist in consciousness, they surely are to be found in the unconscious, where they still exert an influence on behavior. Jung always maintained that what is unconscious cannot be individuated; thus it remains in an undeveloped or primitive state. When it does break through the repression, it tends to disturb and upset one's behavior and even results in abnormal or perverse conduct. In this sense the undeveloped unconscious functions are a potential threat to consciousness.

The assessment of the character of an individual requires, therefore, an estimate of the degree to which each of the attitudes and functions exists in either a differentiated conscious state or an undifferentiated unconscious state. A correct assessment can be obtained only by lengthy observations and penetrating analyses of a person. Usually, such information can only be secured through means of long-term psychoanalysis. In an attempt to shorten the assessment procedures, tests have been devised that purport to measure the intensity of the conscious expression of the attitudes and functions. These tests consist of presenting a person with a list of questions or choices regarding his preferences, interests, and habitual ways of behavior. For example, if he says he would rather stay home and read a book than go to a party this preference is indicative of introversion. If he says he likes to experience a diversity of things this is indicative of a preference for sensation.

V. PRACTICAL CONSIDERATIONS

What determines the pattern of attitudes and functions of a person? Jung believes it is dependent upon inborn factors which manifest themselves very early in the life of the child. This innate pattern is subject to modification by parental and other social influences. Since children of the same family may be of different types and different from the types of their parents, the family pressures brought to bear upon a child to change his orientation may be very great. An introverted feeling mother, for example, may try to convert her extraverted intuitive daughter to her type. Or an extraverted thinking father may want his introverted sensation son to become like him. Consistent with his general position that anything that drastically alters an individual's inborn nature is harmful, Jung believes that such parental influences, if they are effective, often destine the child to become neurotic later in life. The role of the parents, Jung believes, is to respect the rights of the child to develop in the direction of his inner nature, and to offer him every opportunity to do so. Much of the conflict that takes place between parents and children can be traced to the incompatibility of character types.

Jung also points out that one character type may be more favored than other character types during a given period of history. Writing during the first half of the twentieth century, which he felt valued the extraverted types, especially those of thinking and sensation, and depreciated the introverted types, Jung believed introverts bore a heavy burden of social disparagement. Should introverts try to reroute their libido outward in order to conform to the socially accepted stereotype of the "healthy" extravert? If they did, they would be playing a false role which could only result in more frustration and conflict for themselves. On the other hand, if they maintained their introversion in the face of social criticism, they would find themselves in continual conflict with society. To be true to one's nature is, however, the better prescription for mental health.

Also important for a person's mental health is the type of person he or she falls in love with and marries. It cannot be said as a general rule that opposite types will either be more or less compatible than the same types. So much depends on whether the union is complementary or not. An extraverted thinking type who marries an introverted feeling type may obtain satisfaction vicariously by living with someone who expresses the neglected or repressed side of his or her personality. Together they may make a good match. But if the extraverted thinking partner rejects introversion and feeling, the expression of these characteristics in the spouse's behavior will be a continual irritant. Imagine, for example, the possible consequences of a marriage between an uncommunicative introverted feeling type and a thrill-seeking extraverted sensation type, or a union between a flighty extraverted intuitive person and a sober extraverted thinking person. They would certainly get on each other's nerves unless each served to compensate for the other's weakness. And if a person thinks he is going to change his partner's character after they are married, Jung's admonition would be that it is impossible.

Nor is there any guarantee that the same types will be compatible. Consciously they have the same attitudes, interests, and values, which should foster a harmonious relationship. But there is also the danger that they will reinforce each other's dominant attitude and function to such an extent that repression of the other attitude and functions is increased. If this occurs, the repressed attitude and functions will become stronger and more likely to break out in disruptive and destructive behavior. People can also get on each other's nerves by having too many similarities in their personalities.

Harmony is to be established, Jung believed, within the individual and not as a consequence of trying to make a complementary union with another person. Although it is impossible to attain complete psychic harmony in the sense of disposing energy equally among the two attitudes and four functions, inequities can be limited to a minimum by individuating all of the attitudes and functions as completely as possible, and by not severely repressing any one of them. One-sidedness, a popular Jungian theme, can only have harmful and sometimes disastrous consequences. The best friendships and marriages are achieved between fully individuated persons, in which all the attitudes and functions of both their personalities are developed.

Each of the types has a tendency to develop a certain type of neurosis or psychosis. The extraverted feeling type is predisposed to hysteria, and the introverted feeling type to neurasthenia, the symptoms of which are fatigue, exhaustion, and low energy. The sensation types are predisposed to phobias, compulsions, and obsessions. These pathologies result from severe repression, usually as a result of extreme environmental pressures.

It is important for a person to consider his character type when deciding on a vocation. It would never do for an introvert to try to be an automobile salesman or for an extravert to try to be a bookkeeper. A sensation type may make a very fine policeman or fireman but a poor teacher or minister. An intuitive type might do very well as a repair man or "trouble shooter" but not so well as a factory worker engaged in routine, repetitive work. Feeling types should avoid jobs that call for sustained abstract thought, and thinking types should avoid occupations that place a premium on emotional involvement. Unfortunately, due to social pressures, egocentricity, and various other influences, a man may choose a vocation contradictory to his character type. As a result he becomes a victim of unhappiness, dissatisfaction, and emotional disturbance. If he continues to pursue this vocation at the expense of his mental stability, he will surely suffer from a psychological illness which could prove to be fatal. Socrates' famous injunction "Know thyself" bears an important message for all of mankind.

In conclusion, it should be noted that Jung's typology has been severely criticized by psychologists who insist that people do not fit neatly into eight, or eighty, classes. Each individual, they argue, is unique and not a member of a specific class. These criticisms indicate a misunderstanding of Jung's position. He would not argue about the uniqueness of the individual's psyche, which to him was self-evident. What his typology does is to offer a system for characterizing the significant ways in which people differ from one another. The attitudes and functions are in every personality, but they are there in different proportions and at different levels of consciousness and unconsciousness. Some are more individuated than others. It is, above all, a system for describing individual differences, and definitely not a system for reducing every person to one of eight fixed types.

VI. SUMMARY

Jung's typology consists of two attitudes, extraversion and introversion, and four functions, thinking, feeling, sensation, and intuition, making eight types of characters in all. Variations in the degree to which each of the attitudes and functions are consciously developed or remain unconscious and undeveloped can produce a wide range of differences among individuals.

REFERENCES

JUNG, C. G. *Collected Works.* Princeton, N. J.: Princeton University Press.
Vol. 5. *Symbols of Transformation.*

Vol. 6. *Psychological Types.*
Vol. 10. *Civilization in Transition.*
JUNG, C. G. *Man and His Symbols.* Garden City, N. Y.: Doubleday, 1964.

CHAPTER SIX

Symbols and Dreams

Jung contributed elaborately to the study of symbolization processes; he devoted more research and writings to the subject than any other psychologist. Five of his eighteen volumes are devoted exclusively to symbolism in religion and alchemy, and the subject is discussed frequently throughout virtually all of his writings. It would be no exaggeration to say that Jung's two most important concepts are the archetype and the symbol. The two concepts are intimately related. Symbols are the outward manifestations of archetypes. Archetypes can only express themselves through symbols, since the archetypes are deeply buried in the collective unconscious, unknown and unknowable to the individual. Nevertheless, the archetypes are constantly influencing and directing the conscious behavior of the person. It is only by analyzing and interpreting symbols, dreams, fantasies, visions, myths, and art that one can obtain any knowledge of the collective unconscious.

This is exactly what Jung did in one of his earliest volumes, *Symbols of Transformation*. It was this book, written in 1911, that signaled Jung's deviation from the teachings of Freud and that led, within a few years, to a complete separation between the two men. More importantly, it laid the groundwork for Jung's subsequent discoveries in the realm of the psyche.

I. AMPLIFICATION

Symbols of Transformation is a searching analysis of a series of fantasies produced by a young American woman. Jung called the method of analysis that he used in this and succeeding investigations *amplification*. This method requires the analyst to gather all the knowledge he possibly can about a particular verbal element or image. This knowledge may be obtained from a variety of sources: the analyst's own experience and knowledge, information and associations contributed by the person who produced the image, historical references, anthropological and archeological findings, literature, art, mythology, religion, etc.

For example, the young woman wrote a poem entitled "The Moth to the Sun." The poem is about a moth who will die happily if it can gain just "one raptured glance" from the sun. Jung devotes a chapter of 38 pages to amplifying the image of a moth seeking the sun. In the course of the amplification he refers to Goethe's *Faust*, Apuleius's *The Golden Ass*, Christian, Egyptian, and Persian texts, Martin Buber, Thomas Carlyle, Plato, modern poetry, Nietzsche, the hallucinations of a schizophrenic patient, Lord Byron, *Cyrano de Bergerac*, and many other references. It will be seen that the method of amplification requires considerable scholarship and erudition on the part of the analyst. In the course of a conversation with one of the authors of this book, Jung ascribed the vast knowledge he had of multiple subjects to the diversity of patients he treated. Many of these people were highly educated, and Jung had to learn about their specialized fields in order to be able to amplify their dreams and symbolism. For example, a theoretical physicist undergoing a Jungian analysis would express his complexes and archetypes in the terminology and concepts of modern physics.

The goal of amplification is to comprehend the symbolic significance and the archetypal roots of a dream, fantasy, hallucination, painting, or any other human product. Thus, for example, Jung writes concerning the song of the moth:

"Under the symbol of 'moth and sun' we have dug deep down into the historical layers of the psyche, and in the course of our excavations have uncovered a buried idol, the sun-hero, 'young, comely, with glowing locks and fiery crown,' who, forever unattainable to mortal man, revolves around the earth, causing night to follow day, and winter summer, and death life, and who rises again in rejuvenated splendor to give light to new generations. For him the dreamer longs with her very soul, for him the 'soul-moth' burns her wings" (Vol. 5, p. 109). In the sun-hero, we see the representation of an archetype, the product of countless generations of men experiencing the great power and radiance of the sun.

Jung devoted a great deal of attention to alchemy. It is commonly believed that the alchemists of the Middle Ages attempted to convert base metals into gold. Actually, alchemy was a very complex philosophy that expressed itself through chemical experimentation. It was taken very seriously by philosophers and scientists during the Middle Ages, and a vast literature on the subject was produced. Out of it grew the modern science of chemistry.

Jung was attracted to the subject because he felt that the symbolism of alchemical philosophy and experimentation revealed many, if not all, of man's inherited archetypes. With characteristic scholarly zeal, Jung mastered the vast literature of alchemy and wrote two volumes on its significance for psychology.

Psychology and Alchemy is particularly interesting to the psychologist because in it Jung demonstrates how the symbolism of medieval alchemy reappears in the dreams and visions of a person who was undergoing psychoanalysis, during the twentieth century and who knew nothing about alchemy. In one dream a number of people are walking to the left around a square. The dreamer stands at one side. The people say that a gibbon (a species of ape) is to be reconstructed. The square symbolizes the work of the alchemists, which consists of breaking down the original chaotic mass of primal material into four elements preparatory to their being recombined into a more perfect unity. Walking around the square represents this unity. The gibbon stands for a substance that transforms base metal into gold.

According to Jung, the dream signifies that the patient (who stands off to one side of the unifying activity) has permitted his conscious ego to play too dominant a role in his personality and that he has neglected to individuate and express the shadow side of his nature. The patient can achieve inner harmony only by integrating *all* elements of his personality, just as the alchemist could only reach his goal by the proper mixture of basic elements.

In another dream, a glass filled with a jellylike substance is on a table before the dreamer. The glass stands for the apparatus used by alchemists for distillation, and the contents stand for the formless substance which the alchemist tries to turn into the philosopher's stone. This stone has the power of transmuting base metals into gold. The alchemical symbols in this dream indicate that the dreamer is trying or should be trying to transform himself into a more transcendent (integrated) person.

When the dreamer dreams of water, it is said to represent the regenerative power of the alchemist's *aquavitae* or water of life; when he dreams of finding a blue flower, the flower stands for the birthplace of the philosopher's stone; and when he dreams of throwing gold coins on the ground, he is expressing his scorn for the alchemist's ideal of achieving a perfectly unified substance. When the patient draws a wheel, Jung sees a connection between it and the alchemist's wheel, which represents the circulating process within the distillery which was supposed to produce the transformation of materials. In a similar vein, Jung interprets an egg that appears in the patient's dream as the primal material with which the alchemist begins his labors, and a diamond which he also dreams about as the coveted stone.

Throughout all the dreams, there are strong parallels between the symbols employed by the dreamer to represent his problems and his goals, and the symbols used by medieval alchemists to represent their endeavors. The striking feature of these particular dreams is the rather exact portrayal in them of the objects and materials used by alchemy. Because of his knowledge of the alchemy literature Jung was able to point to exact duplications of objects in the dreams in the illustrations found in old alchemical texts. He concluded from this study that the strivings of the medieval alchemists as projected into their chemical experiments and those of the patients are precisely the same. The dreamer was trying to individuate himself in his dreams in order to achieve unity just as the alchemists tried to individuate (transform) matter to obtain a perfect substance. Jung believes that the correspondence of the images of dreams with the tools and practices of alchemy is evidence for the existence of universal archetypes.

Moreover, Jung, who carried on anthropological investigations in Africa and other parts of the world, found the same archetypes expressed in the myths of primitive races.

They are also expressed in religion and art, both modern and primitive. He concluded, "The forms which the [archetypal] experience takes in each individual may be infinite in their variations, but, like the alchemical symbols, they are all variants of certain central types, and these occur universally" (Vol. 12, p. 463).

One of Jung's most appealing essays discusses the symbolism of a "modern myth"—that of flying saucers. Jung does not try to prove whether there are or are not flying saucers. Rather he asks the very psychological question, "Why do so many people believe they have seen flying saucers?" In answering this question—the only one, he acknowledges, that a psychologist is competent to discuss—he demonstrates by means of dreams, myths, art, and historical references that the flying saucer is a symbol of totality. It is a luminous disk, a mandala. It comes to earth from another planet (the unconscious), and contains strange creatures (the archetypes).

This typical Jungian analysis (amplification) is purely psychological; it does not depend upon the reality or unreality of flying saucers. To which one might add, if they are real, then their inventors are dominated by the same unity archetype that motivates the seeing of them by terrestial beings. The reality of the psyche is the only reality that the psychologist is interested in; the reality of the external world is the concern of the physical scientist.

The concern with flying saucers (UFOs or unidentified flying objects), which reached its zenith in the 1950's, was the result of confusion and conflict in the world, according to Jung. People wanted to be freed from the burden of the cold war and international disunity, and to achieve harmony and unity. In times of crisis, Jung points out, new symbols are likely to be devised or old ones revived. In these uncertain and dehumanizing times, for example, some people turn to astrology in order to find their own individuality. Others look to Eastern religion and philosophy, or to primitive Christianity for symbolic representations of selfhood.

II. SYMBOLS

Let us now be more systematic in discussing Jung's theory of symbolism. For Jung, a symbol, whether used in nocturnal dreams or in waking life, serves two major purposes. On the one hand, it represents an attempt to satisfy an instinctual impulse that has been frustrated. This aspect of a symbol corresponds to Freud's notion of the symbol as a disguise for a wish that seeks fulfillment. Sexual and aggressive wishes, which are so frequently inhibited in waking life, account for many of the symbols in dreams.

For Jung, a symbol is more than a disguise. Symbols are also transformations of primitive instinctual drives. They attempt to channel instinctual libido into cultural or spiritual values. This is the familiar idea that literature and the arts, as well as religion, are transmutations of the biological instincts. For example, sexual energy is diverted into the dance as an art form, or aggressive energy is diverted into competitive games.

Jung insists, however, that a symbol or symbolic behavior is not merely a way of displacing instinctual energy from their original objects to substitute ones. That is, dancing is not only a substitution for sexual activity; it is something much more than that.

The essential features of Jung's theory of symbolism are disclosed in this statement by him: "The symbol is not a sign that veils something everybody knows. Such is not its significance; on the contrary, it represents an attempt to elucidate, by means of analogy, something that still belongs entirely to the domain of the unknown or something that is yet to be" (Vol. 7, p. 287). It will be recalled that we discussed the analogy-making feature of symbolization in Chapter Three in connection with the canalization of energy.

What is it that is "as yet completely unknown and only in the process of formation"? It is an archetype buried in the collective unconscious. A symbol, above all, is an attempt to represent an archetype, but the result is always imperfect. Jung contended that man's history is a record of his search for better symbols, that is, for symbols that realize fully and consciously (individuate) the archetypes. In some periods of history, for example, the early Christian era and the Renaissance, many good symbols were born—good in the sense that they fulfilled many sides of man's nature. In other periods, notably the present century, symbolism tends to be sterile and one-sided. Modern symbols, which consist largely of machines, weapons, technology, international corporations, and political systems, are expressions of the shadow and persona, and neglect other aspects of the psyche. Jung very much hoped mankind would create better (unifying) symbols before it destroyed itself in war.

The symbolism of alchemy attracted Jung because he saw in it an effort to encompass all sides of man's nature and to forge opposing forces into a unity. The mandala or magic circle is the chief symbol of this transcendent self.

In the final analysis, symbols are representations of the psyche; they are projections of all aspects of man's nature. They not only try to express the stored-up racially and individually acquired wisdom of mankind but they can also represent levels of development that are predestinations of the individual's future status. Man's destiny, the future evolution of his psyche, is marked out for him by symbols. However, the knowledge contained in a symbol is not directly known to man; he must decipher the symbol by the method of amplification in order to discover its important message.

The two aspects of a symbol, one retrospective and guided by the instincts, the other prospective and guided by the ultimate goals of the transcendent personality, are two sides of the same coin. A symbol may be analyzed using either side of the coin. Retrospective analysis exposes the instinctual basis of a symbol, and prospective analysis reveals the yearnings of mankind for completion, rebirth, harmony, purification, and the like. The former is a causal, reductive type of analysis; the latter a teleological, finalistic type of analysis. Both are necessary for a complete elucidation of the symbol. Jung believed that the prospective character of a symbol has been neglected in favor of the view that a symbol is solely a product of instinctual impulses and wishes striving to assert themselves.

The psychic intensity of a symbol is always greater than the value of the cause that produced the symbol. By this is meant that there is both a driving force and an attracting force behind the creation of a symbol. The push is provided by instinctual energy, the pull by transcendental goals. Neither one alone suffices to create a symbol. Consequently, the psychic intensity of a symbol is the combined sum of causal and finalistic determiners and is therefore greater than the causal factor alone.

III. DREAMS

Jung read Freud's *Interpretation of Dreams* in 1900 soon after it appeared and referred to it several times in his doctoral dissertation published in 1902. But just as Jung's views of the psyche eventually deviated so widely from those of Freud's that Jung disassociated himself from Freudian psychoanalysis and developed his own ideas and concepts, so his views of dreams came to differ sharply from those of the Viennese psychoanalyst.

For Jung, as for Freud, dreams are the clearest expression of the unconscious mind. "Dreams," he wrote, "are impartial, spontaneous products of the unconscious psyche ... they show us the unvarnished natural truth" (Vol. 10. p. 149). By reflecting on our dreams we are reflecting on our basic nature.

Not all dreams are equally useful for this purpose. Many of them are concerned with the day's preoccupations and shed little light on the deeper aspects of the dreamer's psyche. Occasionally, one has a dream that is so remote from one's life, so *numinous* (Jung's favorite word for an intensely moving experience), and so strange and uncanny that it does not seem to belong to the dreamer. It is like a visitation from another world, which in truth it is, the other world being the subterranean one of the unconscious. In ancient times, and even today among some people, such dreams are regarded as messages from the gods or ancestral figures.

These dreams are called "big" dreams by Jung. They occur when there are disturbances and dislocations in the unconscious, often brought on by the ego's failure to deal satisfactorily with the external world. People in psychoanalysis frequently have "big" dreams because the treatment agitates the unconscious. On the basis of the dreams that his German patients told him following the first World War, Jung prophesied that the "blond beast" was ready at any moment to burst out of its underground prison with devastating consequences to the world. This prophecy was made many years before the rise of Hitler.

We have already noted that Jung disagreed with Freud's

fundamental idea that a symbol is a disguised representation of a repressed wish. For Jung, dream symbols, or any other symbols for that matter, are attempts to individuate the anima, persona, shadow, and other archetypes and to unify them into a harmonious, balanced whole. Dreams may indeed dip into the past and revive old memories; more importantly, they are—or at least some of them are—projects for realizing the aims of the developing personality. They point to the future as well as to the past. They are messages to be read and guides to be followed. "The prospective function ... is an anticipation in the unconscious of future conscious achievements, something like a preliminary exercise or sketch, or a plan roughed out in advance. Its symbolic content sometimes outlines the solution of a conflict ..." (Vol. 8, p. 255). Jung warns us, however, not to treat every dream as being prospective, for there are probably only a few that conform to this type.

Looking at them in another way, dreams are compensatory; they try to compensate for the neglected, and consequently undifferentiated, aspects of the psyche, and thereby attempt to bring about a balance that is lacking. "The general function of dreams is to try to restore our psychological balance by producing dream material that reestablishes ... the total psychic equilibrium" (*Man and His Symbols*, 1964, p. 50).

A. DREAM SERIES Jung was probably the first person to suggest that in addition to analyzing single dreams as the Freudians did, one could also analyze a series of dreams recorded over a period of time by an individual. In fact, Jung attached little importance to the interpretation of a single dream and required his patients to keep a careful log of their dreams. The dreams of a series are like the chapters in a book; each chapter adds something new to the total narrative, and taken together they form an interlocking coherent picture of the personality just as the pieces of a jigsaw puzzle form a picture when they are fitted together. Moreover, a dream series reveals the recurrent themes, and thereby the principal preoccupations of the dreaming mind. We have used the dream-series method to good advantage in our investigations of dreams

(Hall, 1966; Hall and Lind, 1970; Bell and Hall, 1971; Hall and Nordby, 1972).

Here are a few examples of the analysis of dream series made from a Jungian orientation. An engineer who kept a record of his dreams over a period of years (he was then in his thirties) dreamed repeatedly of having intimate sexual relations with a number of women friends. Although married, his sexual life was virtually nonexistent, except for frequent masturbation which was accompanied by the same fantasies that he had while he was asleep. Prior to marriage, he had had no sexual relations of any kind, and during his married life he had no affairs with other women, and relations with his wife were increasingly unsatisfactory. At his wife's insistence he had a vasectomy, presumably to prevent them from having any more children.

The numerous sex dreams, many of which were very realistic, detailed, and intense, were compensatory for what he lacked in waking life. It is true they were wish-fulfillments in the Freudian sense, but for a Jungian, they indicated the reason why he was unable to obtain gratification. He had throughout his life inhibited or renounced the shadow side of his personality. He was a hardworking, intellectual person who had adopted a moral code that placed constraints on his natural impulses. Consequently, he was tormented by sexual fantasies during the day and sexual dreams during the night. The dreams were trying to tell him that he could not ignore a part of his nature without crippling his life. This repression did indeed have disastrous effects on his marriage, his work, and his personal relations. His sex dreams had a crude compulsive quality which is characteristic of an undifferentiated shadow.

A young woman who had an unsuccessful marriage often dreamed of fighting with men and of being attacked by them. Her relations with men in waking life were also very unsatisfactory because she fluctuated between docility and dominance. Sometimes she was affectionate, thoughtful, and tender; at other times she was sarcastic, selfish, and argumentative. Jung would point out that such a woman is the victim of her animus, the masculine component in the female personality. Essentially what occurred was a rejection of her own masculinity. She considered it to be the enemy within; a foreign body to be destroyed, although, of course, she could not articulate this consciously.

She could not have satisfactory relations with men in waking life any more than she could in her dreams, because they were, for her, the embodiment of her own hated masculinity. When her animus did assert itself, whether asleep or awake, her behavior overcompensated for the neglect. She became too masculine, that is, too assertive. This was followed by a flight into docility and abject submissiveness. She then became a caricature of femininity just as formerly she was a caricature of masculinity.

Her sexual relations were unsatisfactory because she considered the sex act to be an invasion of her body by the male element. This feeling she was aware of; what she did not know consciously—her dreams knew it, however—is that she feared invasion of her psyche by her own animus. Time and again she had been threatened by her primitive, undeveloped animus. Her bad relations with men were the result of her bad relations with her animus. The essence of Jungian psychology is that a person should always look within the psyche for answers to his relationships with other people, since we project our psychic states on them.

The rejection of her masculinity began in childhood, when her mother subjected her to a constant barrage of criticism and invective directed against males. The image of masculinity that became imprinted on her mind was a hateful one. Experiences with men confirmed this image, and the rejection of her own animus grew stronger.

At the same time, her mother constantly stressed the importance of being "ladylike." This spurious conception of the female psyche became her mask (persona). Appearance displaced nature.

Jung reminds us that external conflicts—in this case, conflicts with men—are always and inevitably the projections of disharmony within the personality. Conflicts cannot be cured by treating the external symptoms; the internal disharmonies must be dealt with in order to ameliorate the externalized conflicts. One cannot, in short, escape the basic reality of the archetypes that constitute the core of the personality. "Everything begins with the individual."

A businessman whose dreams we analyzed solved his anima problem in an unusual way. From an early age, he had recognized that another person, feminine in character, dwelt within him. He even called this other personality by a woman's name. But he also had an equally strong masculine character. The solution consisted of living as a man by day with his business associates, and as a woman when he returned home in the evening from work. His wife not only tolerated the transformation; she encouraged it by showing him how to dress, groom himself, talk, and behave in a feminine manner. They were like two sisters. In his sexual relations with her, he was, however, a man.

From a study of the dreams of a child molester we concluded that he was a child himself. He had never grown up. He was a child who played sexually with other children. In Jungian terms, he was the victim of the child archetype. The child archetype dominated his psyche because he had an overprotective mother and a seductive father.

Jung did not believe in using a *fixed* symbolism or dream-book approach to the interpretation of dreams. So much depends upon the individual circumstances and the condition of the dreamer's mind. The age of the dreamer and his sex and race, for example, must be taken into account when analyzing a particular dream element. The same element may have different meanings for different people, as well as different meanings for the same person at different times. Jung preferred to keep an open mind about the meaning of a dream; he did not try to force it into a preconceived theoretical mold.

Jung believed that in trying to learn the significance of a dream one should stay close to the dream and not go far afield with the dreamer's free associations. Free associations, Jung felt, often permit the dreamer to evade the aim of understanding the dream by bringing up irrelevant material. Amplification of dream elements, on the other hand, keeps the dreamer closely involved with the dream.

When it is realized that Jung, according to his own estimate, analyzed and interpreted no less than 80,000 dreams during his professional lifetime, it is easy to see why he is considered to be one of the greatest dream experts of all time. The same may be said about his knowledge of symbolism, which was exceedingly broad and deep. One should not forget, however, that his study of dreams and symbols led to the discovery of the collective unconscious and its archetypes. This was his preeminent achievement.

REFERENCES

BELL, A. P., and HALL, C. S. *The Personality of a Child Molester: An Analysis of Dreams.* Chicago, Ill.: Aldine-Atherton, 1971.

HALL, C. S. *The Meaning of Dreams.* New York: McGraw-Hill, 1966.

HALL, C. S., and LIND, R. E. *Dreams, Life, and Literature: A Study of Franz Kafka.* Chapel Hill, N. C.: University of North Carolina Press, 1970.

HALL, C. S., and NORDBY, V. J. *The Individual and His Dreams.* New York: New American Library, 1972.

JUNG, C. G. *Collected Works.* Princeton, N. J.: Princeton University Press.
  Vol. 5. *Symbols of Transformation.*
  Vol. 7. *Two Essays on Analytical Psychology.*
  Vol. 8. *The Structure and Dynamics of the Psyche.*
  Vol. 10. *Civilization in Transition.*
  Vol. 12. *Psychology and Alchemy.*

JUNG, C. G. *Man and His Symbols.* Garden City, N. Y.: Doubleday, 1964.

CHAPTER SEVEN

Jung's Place in Psychology

In this final chapter, we would like to discuss Jung's position on some of the issues which are important to psychology and to society. Until quite recently, psychology tried to be a laboratory science like physics and physiology. This meant that psychologists attempted to understand mental phenomena and behavior by performing experiments under controllable laboratory conditions. By varying the conditions systematically, it would be determined that variables were important in producing a particular type of behavior. The goal of scientific psychology is the formulation of general laws of behavior which would be expressed in mathematical terms.

At the same time that psychologists were working to establish a science of psychology, psychiatry was becoming established as a branch of medicine. The task of psychiatry was the treatment of patients who were mentally ill, although soon it became evident that many of those who sought help from psychiatrists were not ill in the usual sense of that word. They were simply unhappy, discontented, anxious human beings. Medicines and surgery were of no help to them.

What the psychiatrist needed was a knowledge of the mind just as the other branches of medicine needed a knowledge of the body. Scientific psychology did not provide them with the appropriate kind of knowledge and understanding of the human mind, which was so necessary for founding the practice of psychiatry. Consequently, they had to become their own psychologists. Instead of gathering information about human behavior and personality from the laboratory experiments they obtained it from within their own consulting rooms. They listened to, observed, questioned, and analyzed everything their patients said and did. They made inferences or interpretations which they checked against their observations. After proceeding in this manner with a number of patients, they began to formulate concepts regarding the psyche, and to fit these concepts together into a general psychological theory.

On the one hand, then, there was a psychology that grew out of the laboratory and on the other hand, a psychology that grew out of the psychiatrist's practice. Recently, these two psychologies have begun to combine to form a single psychology. The formulations of psychiatrists are being tested in the laboratory or in natural settings, and the formulations of scientific psychology are being tried out in the therapeutic situation. It is not an easy task to take ideas out of the clinic and into the laboratory or out of the laboratory into the clinic. The psychotherapist is concerned with the individual and his total personality, and he often feels that the laboratory psychologist is only interested in specific psychological processes like perception, learning, and memory, and in the statistically average man. The laboratory psychologist accuses the therapist of not being scientific and of basing his subjective generalizations on a few "sick" people. Jung's concepts are especially difficult to study in the laboratory, and he has often been charged with being mystical because of his interest in the occult. An answer to this indictment may be contained in the following statement that he wrote in 1930.

"Occultism has enjoyed a renaissance in our times that is without parallel—*the light of the Western mind is nearly darkened by it.* I am not thinking now of our seats of learning and their representatives. As a doctor who deals with ordinary people, I know that the universities have ceased to act as disseminators of light. People are weary of scientific specialization and rationalism and intellectualism. They want to hear truths that broaden rather than restrict, that do not obscure but enlighten, that do not run off them like water but penetrate them to the marrow. *This search is only too likely to lead a large if anonymous public astray*" (Vol. 15, p. 58; emphasis added).

Jung's knowledge of psychology was obtained mainly

from his treatment and contact with patients, although for a time early in his carrer he also performed experiments in the laboratory. He wrote, "I am first and foremost a doctor and practicing psychotherapist, and all my psychological formulations are based on the experiences gained in the hard course of my daily professional work" (Vol. 6, p. xiii).

Jung's psychology also derived sustenance from sources outside of his treatment room. These sources included observations of other cultures and studies of comparative religion and mythology, symbolism, alchemy, and occultism. He made it quite clear, however, that these sources were secondary ones. "The theory of the psyche's structure was not derived from fairytales and myths, but is grounded on empirical observations made in the field of medico-psychological research and was corroborated only secondarily through the study of comparative symbology, in spheres very far removed from ordinary medical practice" (Vol. 9i, p. 239). He felt that the comparative method which is used in history, anthropology, archeology, comparative anatomy, and other disciplines was a perfectly good scientific method.

Jung did not believe, however, that one should be bound to any one method any more than one should be bound to any one theory. He wrote, "Theories in psychology are the very devil. It is true that we need certain points of view for their orienting and heuristic [guiding] value; but they should be regarded as mere auxiliary concepts that can be laid aside at any time. We still know so very little about the psyche that it is positively grotesque to think we are far enough advanced to frame general theories. We have not even established the empirical extent of the psyche's phenomenology [experiences]; how then can we dream of general theories? No doubt theory is the best cloak for lack of experience and ignorance, but the consequences are depressing: [they are] bigotedness, superficiality, and scientific sectarianism" (Vol. 17, p. 7).

And just as he did not adhere exclusively to any one method in making empirical observations, so he did not advocate the exclusive use of any one method of psychotherapy. That is why there is no standard Jungian therapeutic method. He used whatever method or methods seemed appropriate for the particular patient he was treating. Sometimes he employed a Freudian approach, sometimes an Adlerian one, and sometimes methods he himself developed. His own methods included dream interpretation, the method of active imagination in which the patient concentrated on forming images, painting, amplification of symbols, and the word-association test. Also, the number of times he saw a patient each week varied according to the condition of the patient. Whenever possible he tried to reduce the number of visits and encouraged the patient to assume increasing responsibility for his own analysis. Jung's flexibility and open-mindedness was one of his great assets as a therapist and as an investigator of the psyche. He did not want to see analytical psychology become a fixed set of orthodox principles and methods. "The more deeply we penetrate the nature of the psyche, the more the conviction grows upon us that the diversity, the multidimensionality of human nature requires the greatest variety of standpoints and methods in order to satisfy the variety of psychic dispositions" (Vol. 16, p. 9).

Perhaps "the variety of standpoints" of Jungian psychology is one reason why Jungian psychotherapists are not in the majority! The methods set forth by Jung encompass such a diversified knowledge of mankind. More precisely, a Jungian therapist must have a "universal knowledge" of man in order to understand every patient in the proper context. We believe that it is because Jungian psychotherapy is so complex, has so many capabilities, and so many different approaches that it is so valuable.

Jung's views on the nature of science were also very broad. The scientific atmosphere to which Jung was exposed as a student was permeated by the idea of *causality*. Everything had its cause. In psychotherapy, this meant that one tried to locate the cause of the patient's present difficulties in his past life. Freud's insistence on the priority of childhood traumas in causing adult neuroses exemplified the causal viewpoint. Jung did not reject the idea of causality. Instead he also recognized the validity of another scientific orientation. This orientation is called *teleology* or *finalism*. As applied in psychology, it means, in effect, that man's present behavior is determined by the future. Future goals, as well as past events, need to be taken into consideration in understanding a person's behavior. Many of Jung's ideas regarding the development of the psyche are finalistic in the sense that they are goals—individuation, integration, and selfhood, for instance—toward which the developing personality is aimed. There is intentionality in behavior, although it is not necessarily always manifested in consciousness. Even dreams serve a prospective function; they are images of the future lines of development as often as they are memory images of the past.

Jung felt that it was necessary to adopt both attitudes, causality and teleology, in psychology. He wrote, "On the one hand it [the mind] gives a picture of the remnants and traces of all that has been, and on the other, but expressed in the same picture, the outlines of what is to come, in so far as the psyche creates its own future" (Vol. 3, pp. 184-185).

Teleology was not and still is not an acceptable idea to many scientists, but as we have seen, Jung was not influenced by consensus. He was always ready to consider any idea, no matter how unpopular it might be, and to apply it in his work. Jung was a pragmatist. If an idea was effective in helping him to understand and to benefit his patients, he used it.

Jung pointed out that, after all, causality and finalism are arbitrary modes of thinking employed by the scientist for ordering observable phenomena. Causality and teleology are not themselves found in nature.

Jung also pointed out another practical value of the finalistic attitude when working with patients. A purely causal attitude is likely to produce feelings of resignation and despair in a patient, since from the standpoint of causality he is a prisoner of his past. The damage has already been done, and it is difficult and sometimes impossible to undo this damage. The finalistic attitude offers the patient hope and something to work toward.

Late in his life, Jung proposed a principle which was neither causality or finalism. He called it *synchronicity*. This principle applies to events that occur together in time but that are not the cause of one another; for example, when a thought corresponds with an objective event. Nearly everyone has experienced such coincidences. One is thinking of a person and the person appears, or a letter is received from him, or one dreams about the illness or death of a friend or relative and later hears the event took place at the exact time of the dream. Jung points to the vast literature on mental telepathy, clairvoyance, and other types of paranormal phenomena as evidence for the necessity of invoking a synchronistic principle in psychology. He believed that many of these experiences, which are so mystifying when they occur, cannot be explained as chance coincidences; instead they suggest that there is another kind of order in the universe in addition to that described by causality. He applied synchronicity to the concept of archetypes, and argued that an archetype can express itself psychically within a person at the same time that it is expressed physically in the external world. The archetype does not cause both events, rather one event parallels the other.

Psychologists, in particular those who work with patients, are likely to become social critics. The reason for this is that the faults of society are clearly revealed and magnified in the lives of people who need and seek psychological treatment. Jung, as we have noted before, could be an impassioned critic of contemporary society. Sometimes his feelings were very pessimistic; then he expressed his views with biting sarcasm. Here is one such example.

"What have all our cultural achievements led to? The fearful answer is there before our eyes: man has been delivered from no fear, a hideous nightmare lies upon the world. So far reason has failed lamentably, and the very thing that everybody wanted to avoid rolls on in ghastly progression. Man has achieved a wealth of useful gadgets, but, to offset that, he has torn open the abyss, and what will become of him now—where can he make a halt? After the last World War we hoped for reason; we go on hoping. But already we are fascinated by the possibilities of atomic fission and promise ourselves a Golden Age—the surest guarantee that the abomination of desolation will grow to limitless dimensions. And who or what is it that causes all this? It is none other than that harmless (!), ingenious, inventive, and sweetly reasonable human spirit who unfortunately is abysmally unconscious of the demonism that still clings to him. Worse, this spirit does everything to avoid looking himself in the face, and we all help him like mad. Only, heaven preserve us from psychology—*that* depravity might lead to self-knowledge! Rather let us have wars, for which somebody else is always to blame, nobody seeing that all the world is driven to do just what all the world flees from in terror" (Vol. 9i, p. 253). This was written in 1948; it might have been written today were Jung still alive.

Jung was not always in such a pessimistic mood. He had worked with enough patients who managed to salvage their lives from the bottom of the abyss to know that the individual can, despite his inner demon and its projection on the world, achieve fortitude and rectitude. "The principle aim of psychotherapy," Jung wrote, "is not to transport the patient to an impossible state of happiness but to help him acquire steadfastness and philosophical patience in the face of suffering" (Vol. 16, p. 81). But of all Jung's utterances on the question of man, the following one probably expresses most eloquently the courage-to-be.

"Personality is the supreme realization of the innate idiosyncrasy of a living being. It is an act of high courage flung in the face of life, the absolute affirmation of all that constitutes the individual, the most successful adaptation to the universal conditions of existence coupled with the greatest possible freedom for self-determination" (Vol. 17, p. 171).

What is the future of Jungian psychology? Will it become a major influence in psychology, which it is not at the present time? Will it have an increasing impact upon the world of ideas? Or will it sink into the oblivion of a footnote in history books? Predictions are risky matters. We have already stated our opinion that Jung's ideas are receiving more attention, especially from young people. Whether this is a transitory fad that will pass or whether it presages a more permanent trend in people's thinking it is impossible to say. We hope that the latter will prove to be correct. Prophecies are sometimes self-fulfilling, which means that the mere fact of stating a prophecy causes it to become true. We earnestly hope our prophecy will be self-fulfilling because we feel that Jung's writings are a seedbed of important ideas, waiting to be recognized by mankind.

Reading Jung is a unique experience. This may not be

recognized at first, but it surely will be after one has read some of his articles and books. It will suddenly dawn on the reader that this solitary man Jung wrote with logic and common sense, and with passion and compassion, about the basic truths of the human spirit. Again and again, the reader will experience a "shock of recognition"; he will recognize truths he has known but which he has not been able to express in words. He will also be astounded, as we have been, by the number of Jung's ideas that anticipated those of later writers. Many of the new trends in psychology and related fields are indebted to Jung, who first gave them their direction.

Jung's writings are an inexhaustible fount of wisdom and inspiration which one can return to repeatedly to learn something new about himself and about the world. That is why it is a uniquely enriching and refreshing experience to read Jung.

REFERENCES

JUNG, C. G. *Collected Works.* Princeton, N. J.: Princeton University Press.
Vol 3. *The Psychogenesis of Mental Disease.*
Vol 6. *Psychological Types.*
Vol. 9i. *The Archetypes and the Collective Unconscious.*
Vol. 15. *The Spirit in Man, Art, and Literature.*
Vol. 16. *The Practice of Psychotherapy.*
Vol. 17. *The Development of Personality.*

A Guide for Reading Jung

The first problem the student encounters when he decides to read about Jung's analytical psychology is where to begin reading, and in what order the reading should follow thereafter. The collected works of Jung in English translation fill nineteen volumes, and these volumes do not include all of his published writings. For example, they do not contain his autobiography, *Memories, Dreams, Reflections*, nor his last published work, *Man and His Symbols*, nor the privately printed *Septem Sermones ad Mortuos* ("Seven Sermons on the Dead"). It would be unwise to start reading at random in the collected writings because many of the subjects are extremely specialized, and would not interest the beginning reader.

Where should one begin? The following suggestions may prove to be helpful. They presuppose no extensive knowledge of psychology. When paperbound editions of the suggested readings are available, we have noted this and have given the name of the publisher. The collected works are published by the Princeton University Press. (In England they are published by Routledge and Kegan Paul.)

We feel that the best introductory approach to Jung can be obtained by reading his *Memories, Dreams, Reflections*. It is available in a paperbound edition published by Vintage Books, a division of Random House. Our second suggestion is the essay by Jung entitled "Approaching the Unconscious," which was written for the book *Man and His Symbols* published in 1964 by Doubleday. There is a paperbound edition published by Dell. This book, which also contains chapters written by other prominent analytical psychologists, is profusely illustrated, and Jung's chapter is a model of clarity. We recommend these two writings of Jung because they were written for the general reader and because they constitute a final statement of his views since they were written near the end of his life.

For more extensive readings of Jung, we suggest the following group of writings in the collected works.

Vol. 6. *Psychological Types.*
Chapter X, "General Description of the Types," pp. 330-407.
Chapter XI, "Definitions," pp. 408-486.
Vol. 7. *Two Essays on Analytical Psychology* (paperbound edition: World Publishing Co.).
"The Psychology of the Unconscious," especially pp. 40-117.
"The Relations between the Ego and the Unconscious."
Vol. 8. *The Structure and Dynamics of the Psyche.*
"On the Nature of the Psyche" (paperbound edition: Princeton University Press).
"The Stages of Life."
Vol. 9, Part I. *The Archetypes and the Collective Unconscious.*
"Archetypes of the Collective Unconscious."
"The Concept of the Collective Unconscious."
"Concerning the Archetypes, with Special Reference to the Anima Concept."
Vol. 12. *Psychology and Alchemy.*
Parts I and II, pp. 1-223.

The foregoing references should provide a solid basis of knowledge concerning Jung's analytical psychology. Many of these articles are reprinted in a paperbound volume entitled *The Portable Jung,* published by Viking Press.

For the reader who wishes to learn Jung's views on a particular subject, the following is a topical guide to the works.

The psychology of primitive man
"Archaic Man," Vol. 10, pp. 50-73.
The psychology of women
"Women in Europe," Vol. 10, pp. 113-133.
The psychology of Americans
"The Complications of American Psychology," Vol. 10, pp. 502-514.

The psychology of religion
  Vol. 11, especially "Psychology and Religion," pp. 5-105, a series of lectures delivered at Yale University in 1937. (These lectures appear in a paperbound edition: Yale University Press.)

Yoga, Zen Buddhism, and I Ching
  Vol. 11, pp. 529-608.

Alchemy
  Vols. 12, 13, and 14.

The psychology of art and literature
  Vol. 15, pp. 65-141. (Paperbound edition: *The Spirit in Man, Art, and Literature*, Princeton University Press.)

Psychotherapy
  Vol. 15, pp. 65-141.

Education
  "Analytical Psychology and Education," Vol. 17, pp. 65-132. (Paperbound edition: Princeton University Press.)

Dreams
  Vol. 8, pp. 237-297.

Astrology
  Vol. 8, pp. 453-483.

Mandala
  Vol. 9, Part I, pp. 355-390.

Extrasensory perception
  Vol. 8, pp. 421-450.

Word-association Test
  Vol. 2.

Freud.
  Vol. 4.

Occult phenomena
  Vol. 1, pp. 3-88.

Schizophrenia (dementia praecox)
  Vol. 2.

We would like to make one final reading suggestion, which illustrates how Jung approaches a psychological problem: "Flying Saucers: A Modern Myth of Things Seen in the Sky" (Vol. 10, pp. 309-433). There is a paperbound edition published by New American Library. Jung has written many more important books and articles than this one, but none of them reveals so clearly the insight Jung uses when confronted with such a controversial issue as flying saucers. It is a pleasurable article to read.

Collected Works of C. G. Jung

These nineteen volumes were edited by Sir Herbert Read, Michael Fordham, and Gerhard Adler. The executive editor was William McGuire. R. F. C. Hull was the translator. They are published by Princeton University Press in the United States and by Routledge and Kegan Paul in Great Britain.

1. *Psychiatric Studies*
2. *Experimental Researches*
3. *The Psychogenesis of Mental Disease*
4. *Freud and Psychoanalysis*
5. *Symbols of Transformation*
6. *Psychological Types*
7. *Two Essays on Analytical Psychology*
8. *The Structure and Dynamics of the Psyche*
9. Part i. *The Archetypes and the Collective Unconscious*
   Part ii. *Aion: Researches into the Phenomenology of the Self*
10. *Civilization in Transition*
11. *Psychology and Religion: West and East*
12. *Psychology and Alchemy*
13. *Alchemical Studies*
14. *Mysterium Coniunctionis*
15. *The Spirit in Man, Art, and Literature*
16. *The Practice of Psychotherapy*
17. *The Development of Personality*
18. *Miscellany*
19. *Bibliography and Index*

Recommended Readings

DRY, AVIS M. *The Psychology of Jung.* New York: Wiley, 1961.

FORDHAM, FRIEDA *An Introduction to Jung's Psychology.* London: Penguin Books, 1953.

JACOBI, JOLANDE *Complex, Archetype, Symbol in the Psychology of C. G. Jung.* New York: Pantheon Books, 1959.

PROGOFF, I. *Jung's Psychology and Its Social Meaning.* New York: Julian, 1953.

SERRANO, M. C. *Jung and Herman Hesse.* London: Routledge and Kegan Paul, 1966.

WEHR, G. *Portrait of Jung.* New York: Herder and Herder, 1971.

INDEX

INDEX